ᵀᴴᴱ BETTER-WRITING
CENTER

SHSAT
PRACTICE TESTS
TJHSST EDITION
2016 UPDATE

By Won Suh, J.D.

This book is dedicated to my loving parents for their unwavering support and patience. This book is also dedicated to my past, present, and future students for the pain and suffering they had to endure, are presently enduring, and will inevitably endure, with me as their teacher.

Dear Student,

Thank you for purchasing this workbook, as you begin or continue preparing for the SHSAT or Thomas Jefferson High School for Science and Technology (TJHSST) admissions test. It means a lot to me that you did. I took great, painstaking care to craft the very best practice tests for you.

Many of you are already qualified enough to be offered a place in one of the top high schools in America, even without additional practice. But some of you are so committed to excellence that you will go above and beyond what's required of you. And that alone is worth my having written this book—students like you make this book worth my time. And it is precisely because I knew highly motivated and gifted students would buy this book that I did the very best job I could with every problem and question. (Some of the passages took me days just to research, let alone write. The same is true of the scrambled paragraphs. As you take these practice tests, I hope you will notice how much time and effort I spent in developing the tests.)

That said, I will offer a word of caution. You may find these practice tests more difficult than the majority of the practice questions you'll find available elsewhere on the market. Please don't get discouraged if your performance on these tests is not up to your expectations. These tests will not necessarily accurately reflect how you will do on the actual SHSAT or TJHSST admissions test. I made these problems more difficult in order to increase your chances of doing well on the admissions test you will take, should you go through this book and understand or master—not just do for the sake of doing or go over nonchalantly—every problem in this book.

Furthermore, this book was not designed to be a comprehensive study guide or review book, so please keep that in mind. The purpose of this book is to provide you with additional practice opportunities; in other words, it was designed to complement the study materials you will undoubtedly pick up from a mainstream commercial publisher.

God bless, and I hope you the very best in your all of your future endeavors. Should you ever need to contact me, my email address is available to you below. I will do my best to get back to you.

Yours truly,

Won Suh
President & Director
The Better Writing Center
Email: won.suh@betterwritingcenter.com

2014 Update: In this update, I fixed some typographical errors, included some pieces of information that I had inadvertently omitted before, updated information about the TJ admissions process, and included new SIS prompts.

2016 Update: In this update, I included essay prompts similar to those asked in 2015 and this year.

CONTENTS

FREE CONSULTATION

Thank you for your purchase. Your purchase entitles you to a complimentary hour of in-person private tutoring or academic consultation.* Just bring this book!

SCHEDULE YOUR CONSULTATION TODAY
won.suh@betterwritingcenter.com

*This offer is subject to scheduling and availability limitations and will be honored on a first come, first serve basis.

TUTORING OFFERED

LEARN FROM THE BEST. LEARN FROM THE AUTHOR.

TESTING	MATHEMATICS	SCIENCE	WRITING
CogAT	Algebra 1 & 2	Biology	School Assignments
SSAT	Geometry	Chemistry	AP History DBQs
SHSAT	Trigonometry	Physics	Personal Statements
ACT	Pre-calculus	Computer Science	Application Essays
SAT	AP Calculus AB & BC		

FIND THE BETTER WRITING CENTER

THE BETTER WRITING CENTER
7369 McWhorter Place
Suite 402
Annandale, Virginia 22003

TJHSST

ADMISSIONS OVERVIEW

Admissions Process

Introduction

The TJHSST admissions process consists of two rounds of student selection. The first round or cut determines the semifinalists for further consideration and is based on the applicants' test scores and grade point averages. The second cut narrows down the pool of semifinalists to the finalists, or those who are offered admission to TJHSST. The second cut criteria are: an essay, teacher recommendations, the math and verbal scores of the admissions test, grade point average, and student information sheet. For a more detailed breakdown of the decision processes, read below. (All of the information on this page can be found on the TJHSST admissions webpage, which I've listed in the Resources chapter at the end of the workbook.)

Semifinalist Selection

As mentioned above, two criteria will be considered for the first cut: your GPA and test score. A sliding scale will be used to determine what balance of GPA and test score is sufficient for the first cut. In other words, the higher your GPA is, the lower your test score can be, and vice versa.

Grade Point Average

Only the core subjects (math, English, science, and social studies) are factored into your GPA, for the purpose of TJHSST admissions. (If you take a foreign language course for high school credit, then that will count towards your GPA as well.) The admissions committee will look at your final grades from 7th grade and first quarter grades from 8th grade. Your 7th grade GPA will be given four times the weight that will be given to your 8th grade first quarter GPA.

Test Score

For the semifinalist selection round, the admissions committee will look at your total test score, which is comprised of the verbal and math sections. Note, though, that you must score at least 30 out of 50 questions on the math section to be considered for semifinalist selection. Thus, even if you scored a perfect on the verbal section and your GPA is perfect, you will not be selected as a semifinalist if your math score on the admission test is 29 or lower.

Sliding Scale

GPA and test score are balanced against each other to determine eligibility for selection as a semifinalist. If your GPA is at least 3.0, but lower than 3.25, a test score of at least 70 (out of 100) is required; if your GPA is at least 3.25, but lower than 3.50, a test score of at least 65 is required; and if your GPA is 3.50 or higher, a test score of at least 60 is required. **Students with a GPA lower than 3.0 cannot qualify.** GPA is not rounded up or down.

FINALIST SELECTION

The finalist selection process has undergone a significant overhaul for the 2013-2014 admissions year (or, for the Class of 2018). The information page regarding the finalist selection process no longer contains the breakdown of the weights given to each of the following criteria, whereas it used to:

- **Essay**

  Gone are two essays students were required to write, in addition to the Student Information Sheet (SIS). Now, students only have to write one essay, in addition to the SIS. And instead of writing the essays on the day of the multiple choice test, only semifinalists are required to write the essay. The essay has a maximum character count of 3700 (approximately 800 words).

- **Student Information Sheet (SIS)**

  This is a collection of responses that TJ requires of its semifinalists and is separate from the essays. They are designed to shed more insight about who you are as a person, such as what your interests, talents, and ambitions are.

  Semifinalists will write 3 SIS prompts. Each response can contain up a maximum of 1650 characters (approximately 380 words).

- **Teacher Recommendations**

  Two teacher recommendations are required. In the 2012-2013 admissions cycle, even extra-curricular coaches and instructors could write recommendations, but this has been since removed, so I would not recommend even trying.

- **Admissions Test Math and Verbal Scores (Again)**

  Up until the 2012-2013 admissions cycle, only the math test score was considered in the finalist selection process.

- **Overall GPA (Again)**

  Up until the 2012-2013 admissions cycle, only the math and science GPA was considered in the finalist selection process. Now, the overall GPA is used again, as it was in the semifinalist selection process.

THE TEST

INTRODUCTION

The TJ admissions test, as it is commonly referred to (I'll refer to it as the TJAT for further brevity), is a modified version of the Specialized High Schools Admissions Test (SHSAT), which is administered by New York City. The two tests are very similar in content, but there are some differences, which you should be acutely aware of as you prepare for the test, especially considering that the vast majority of preparation guides and materials available commercially are for New York City's admissions test and not specifically for admissions to TJHSST. (Similarly, if you've purchased this book to prepare for the SHSAT, then you should be aware of these differences, as well, as this book was specifically adapted to prepare students for the TJAT.)

COMPARISON CHART OF THE TESTS

	TJAT	SHSAT
Test Duration	**2 Hours**	**2.5 Hours**
Verbal Suggested Time	60 Minutes	75 Minutes
Math Suggested Time	60 Minutes	75 Minutes
Multiple Choice Test Questions	**95 (100 Points)**	**95 (100 Points)**
Verbal: Scrambled Paragraphs	5 (10 points)	5 (10 points)
Verbal: Logical Reasoning	15	10
Verbal: Reading	25	30
Mathematics	50	50
Mathematics Formula Sheet Provided	Yes	No
Reading Passages	**5**	**5**
Questions Per Passage	5	6

TESTED CONTENT

The TJAT and SHSAT are very similar, but the official practice tests for New York City schools' SHSAT seem to be marginally more difficult than the official practice test for the TJAT.

Since there are no officially administered tests available to the public (not to my knowledge), the best I could do was analyze the official TJAT practice test and provide a breakdown of the question types accordingly, in the chart below. (I did not prepare one for the NYC SHSAT practice tests because this book is geared towards those seeking admission to TJHSST and did not want to distract from the focus of those students' intended purpose.)

QUESTION TYPES	NUMBER OF QUESTIONS
Verbal: Scrambled Paragraphs – 10 Points	**5 Paragraphs, No Partial Credit**
Verbal: Logical Reasoning – 15 Points	**15**
Logic Number	2
Logic Statement	2
Sets & Comparison	4
Position/Order	5
Sentence Decoding	2
Verbal: Reading – 25 Points	**25**
Main Idea/Purpose	5 (1 for each passage)
Identifying Details	16
Inference/Assumption	4
Math – 50 Points	**50**
Numbers and Their Properties	18
Number Theory	*4*
Arithmetic Operations	*4*
Place Value	*2*
Fraction, Decimal, Percent	*5*
Factors and Multiples	*2*
Comparison and Conversion	5
Ratio and Proportion	*3*
Scale Conversion	*2*
Algebra	13
Solving for a Variable or Unknown	*10*
Polynomial Operations	*2*
Algebraic Substitution	*1*
Geometry	8
Angles	*1*
Perimeter/Circumference	*1*
Area/ Volume	*5*
Coordinates	*1*
Miscellaneous	6
Rate	*1*
Probability	*2*
Statistics	*3*
Word Problems	20
Graphs & Charts	2
Number Lines	2
Figures & Shapes	9

The Essays

On test day, you will have to write two essays. Typically in the past, these prompts have involved ethics, science and technology, or a combination of ethics and science and technology.

These essays are designed to see how well you write and organize your thoughts and to see how your mind works and what you think about certain issues.

Generally, there is no right or wrong answer to these questions. I would advise against stating things that would reflect on you badly as a student and person, however. For instance, do not be cold and heartless for the sake of being cold and heartless, if you are asked to make a tough ethical decision. That's not to say you can't take the seemingly cold and heartless route, if there is one, but you should justify your decision to show your good intentions for making that choice.

Essay Components

Every good essay contains an introduction, body, and conclusion. Chances are, you've heard of the 5 paragraph essay, and it exists for good reason—it is a logical and well-presented method of communication. For the TJ admissions test, however, you may not have the luxury of time or space to write five paragraphs; for most students, I recommend writing four.

1. *Introductory Paragraph*

The introduction must contain the thesis or central point you will present or argue. This is non-negotiable. It should have a "hook" or lead-in sentence(s) to transition the reader to the thesis statement and a "roadmap" sentence that will alert the reader to what supports the author will use to support the thesis. I used the word *should* because the hook and roadmap are important, but their omission can be condoned or tolerated if the rest of your essay is well-written, at least for the typical middle school essay.

A. Core Ideas

Your essay must address the core issues raised by the prompts. To put it simply, the core issues ask, "What is the essay *really* about?" By answering the core issues, you are formulating your essay's thesis argument or central point. Your essay should focus on, address, and develop the core issues and the core issues only in your body paragraphs. (Some prompts may involve multiple core issues.) It is important that you not go off on issues/topics/ideas that are merely tangential to the core issues.

That's not to say there aren't auxiliary points that you could tie in to your essay, as long as those secondary points advance your essay in a meaningful way. If the secondary discussion strays from the main point or idea and is ultimately unnecessary, then get rid of it.

EXAMPLE

Consider the following prompt: "You are leading a team of scientists that is conducting research to find cures and treatments for various types of cancer. You have the option of choosing to collaborate with another country's team of scientists that is conducting similar research. Would you opt to work independently of the other team (which may take longer but bring more prestige and financial payoff to your team) or to work with the other country's team (which may bring earlier but shared success)? Include your reasons and ramifications of your choice."

What are the core issues here? Here, the core issue is the comparative advantage of pursuing honor/prestige over saving people's lives, or vice versa, depending on which side you choose to argue. Honor/prestige and saving people's lives should be the *only* issues you discuss. You should not discuss ideas that are tangential to the core issues. For instance, you should not discuss what roadblocks and obstacles, i.e., cooperation problems, language barriers, etc., may arise when two teams have to work together. This also means you should not discuss the possible tangential benefits that may arise when two countries work together, such as improved international relations. (Not being able to identify and focus solely on the core issues is a problem almost all of my previous students have repeatedly had, and it is a problem that I expect the majority of my future students to have as well.)

---

2. *Body Paragraphs*

The body paragraphs are where you provide support for your thesis.

A. AVOID GENERALIZATIONS

Avoid generalizations and hypothetical examples when possible. For instance, consider the simple but meaningful prompt, "Is lying always bad?" It may be tempting to argue that lying is bad as a matter of common sense. The fallacy of arguing that lying is bad as a matter of common sense is that common sense is relative; it depends on the facts of the situation in which you may have to lie.

B. ARGUE FACTS

For instance, if you are lying to protect someone from harm, is lying bad? Wouldn't common sense dictate that lying isn't bad in such cases? As you can see, common sense depends on the situation's context. Thus, when you argue a point, argue context and facts, not just common sense; provide details and facts, not generalizations.

3. *Conclusion*

The conclusion is a concise recapitulation of the thesis and the points made thereafter. The conclusion, while important, is the least important paragraph in your essay. Thus, if you are really pressed for time, or if you're running out of space, consider foregoing the conclusion. It's better to have a strong introduction and body paragraphs without a conclusion than to have a weaker overall essay just so you can include a concluding paragraph.

OTHER WRITING TIPS

1. *Cadence and Flow*

When you write, consider cadence. Good writing is rarely abrupt, unless done intentionally for emphasis or to convey emotion. (This is why transitions are important.) The successful writer lures his or her readers into a rhythmic lullaby, and this is precisely what the cadence is. The complexity of grammar and the difficulty of diction are largely irrelevant in establishing cadence. It is very possible to use simple words and relatively simple sentences to establish cadence. Ask yourself, "Do my words and sentences flow nicely, or do they sound dry, mechanical, or grating?"

Flow is also important to writing. One idea should lead to the next without digressions and distractions. (In essay writing, in particular, maintaining logical flow helps prevent unnecessary diversions away from developing the core issues.) Furthermore, you should not repeat yourself unnecessarily. Think of your writing as a taxi cab—your mission is to take your readers from point A to point B using the shortest, but most pleasant, route possible. You can't do that if you digress or add unnecessary details.

2. *Diction Matters*

Simply, diction is word choice. When you can, use verbs and nouns in place of adjectives and adverbs. Compare the following sentences:

The child ran away as fast he could because he was very frightened.

vs.

The child fled in terror.

Note the impact of the words. The second sentence is much more effective in conveying the urgency and fear than the first. *A corollary: avoid verbiage.*

3. *Don't Try to Sound Too Smart*

This tip ties into the one above it, but it is different enough that it deserves its own space. As a writing instructor, I have seen countless writers (particularly scholars) try too hard to sound unnecessarily smart. It's one thing to use advanced vocabulary and another thing entirely to convolute your writing. The problem with trying to sound too smart is that you force yourself out of your element as a writer. The resulting unnaturalness of your writing in turn leads to awkwardness, dryness, a lack of focus, and redundancy. Your writing may be problematic enough as it is; you don't need to hamper it further. Compare the following sentences:

I enjoy enlightening myself by studying the field of mathematics due to its utilization of the mental faculties of logic and reasoning.

vs.

I enjoy math because it involves logical reasoning.

4. *Practice*

Writing isn't something most people are able to master in their lifetimes. Practice will, however, make you a better writer, if you practice correctly.

A. WORD LIMITS

One way to practice is by rewriting your pieces, i.e., essays and short stories, with a self-imposed word limit. Try to reduce your word count by 20-25% with every revision, <u>without sacrificing on content or meaning</u>, until you absolutely cannot cut out any more words.

B. THESAURUS

Another good tool is the thesaurus. Used correctly, it will help you develop into a more efficient and vibrant writer. Use the thesaurus to help you find substitute words and improve your diction. Be forewarned, though, that the thesaurus is double-edged sword. The danger in using a thesaurus is that, if you're not careful or if you're lazy, you may make your writing worse because the thesaurus lumps together related words but does not distinguish between nearly identical synonyms and substitute words that have different shades of color. Also, some words double as nouns and verbs that have completely unrelated meanings.

C. INTRODUCTORY PARAGRAPHS

If nothing else, practice writing introductory paragraphs repeatedly. Your introduction, if done correctly, will serve as the outline for the rest of your essay and will help you formulate your arguments and support. The introduction is by far the most important paragraph of the entire essay.

Note: For practice directly relevant to the essays you will write as part of the TJAT, see the chapter titled "Resources," in which you will find over 30 essay practice prompts to help you.

the TESTS

SHSAT
TJHSST EDITION
TEST 1

PART 1 — VERBAL

Suggested Time — 60 Minutes
45 QUESTIONS

SCRAMBLED PARAGRAPHS
PARAGRAPHS 1-5

DIRECTIONS: The purpose of this section is to organize sentences into the best six-sentence paragraphs possible. For each paragraph, the first sentence is provided, but the remaining five are presented in random or no particular order. Re-order and organize these five sentences, if necessary, to create the **most** logical paragraph. Each paragraph is worth **two** points, whereas every other question type in this test is worth one. Partial credit will not be given.

Blanks have been provided to help you keep track of the position of each sentence in the paragraph. For instance, if you think a sentence follows the first, given sentence, write "2" in the blank next to it; write "3" next to the sentence that you believe follows "2"; and so on. When you believe you have arranged the sentences correctly, transfer your response to your answer sheet.

Paragraph 1

While most vertebrates are relatively easy to classify as mammal, fish, bird, reptile, or amphibian, some seem to defy ready classification.

___ **Q.** Even more bizarre, despite largely having mammalian bodies, the female platypus lays eggs and the males are equipped with poisonous stingers on the heels of their hind feet.

___ **R.** The platypus, however, would not be a platypus if it permitted such easy conclusions—in addition to its birdlike traits, the platypus also has distinctly mammalian traits, such as a beaver's tail and an otter's body and fur.

___ **S.** It would be easy to conclude, just from its duck's bill and webbed feet alone, that the platypus belongs to the class of birds.

___ **T.** Despite its various oddities which make it difficult to categorize, the platypus is undeniably mammal; after all, it is a warm-blooded vertebrate that has hair to cover its skin, and the females have mammary glands with which they nourish their young.

___ **U.** One such animal is the platypus, which, much to the bewilderment of early scientists, possesses the traits of animals of several different classes—it is perhaps the case, then, that the platypus stood at the evolutionary juncture of several classes of animals.

CONTINUE ▶

Paragraph 2

Everyone knows who the great Thomas Alva Edison is because he remains one of the greatest and most prolific inventors in history.

 Q. Having arrived at Edison's business place penniless, Barnes agreed to do whatever was necessary to earn himself a chance to work alongside the great Edison—he would work as a janitor for years before any semblance of opportunity presented itself.

R. It is hard to imagine, then, that a mere five years before Barnes started out as a member of Edison's sales force, Barnes could not even afford railroad fare to Orange, New Jersey, where Thomas Edison was headquartered.

S. In fact, the only practical way he could and did get to Thomas Edison was by freight train; in doing so, he burned all his bridges and abandoned his life to start another anew.

T. Lesser known, possibly by orders of magnitude, is Edwin Barnes, who made a name for himself as one of Thomas Edison's most successful business associates and salespeople.

U. Many would consider the lengths to which Barnes went to work with Edison to be reckless, but Barnes was a man possessed—his desire to work with Edison was no ordinary desire: it was a tangible, burning desire that paid off magnificently in the end.

Paragraph 3

For better or worse, whether parents like it or not, video games have become firmly entrenched in our culture.

 Q. To shed some perspective on just how rooted video games have become in our society, take, for instance, the year 2009, in which it was estimated that the video game industry generated approximately $60.4 billion.

 R. Two decades later, in 1972, Magnavox introduced the world's first home game console, the Odyssey, which was able to play 12 games, including *Ping-Pong*.

 S. It all started with the very first video game—or at least the very first documented video game—*Noughts and Crosses*, which was created in 1952 by Alexander Shafto Douglas as part of his doctoral dissertation.

T. Of course, the video game industry did not become a multibillion dollar industry overnight—such growth took several decades.

U. Fast forward 40 years to photorealistic games whose production costs often rival those of blockbuster Hollywood films, and it is almost unfathomable that, as technology evolves, so too will the video game landscape—what more evolution could there be?

CONTINUE ▶

Paragraph 4

Though we live in a world of high-speed internet access today, the internet in its infancy was simply an evolution of telephony.

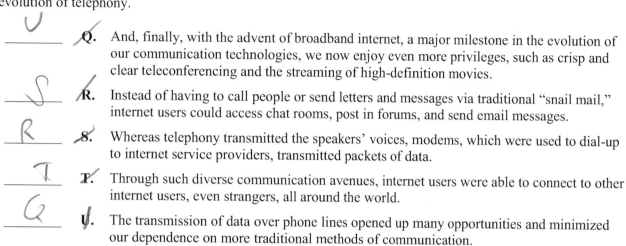

_____ **Q.** And, finally, with the advent of broadband internet, a major milestone in the evolution of our communication technologies, we now enjoy even more privileges, such as crisp and clear teleconferencing and the streaming of high-definition movies.

_____ **R.** Instead of having to call people or send letters and messages via traditional "snail mail," internet users could access chat rooms, post in forums, and send email messages.

_____ **S.** Whereas telephony transmitted the speakers' voices, modems, which were used to dial-up to internet service providers, transmitted packets of data.

_____ **T.** Through such diverse communication avenues, internet users were able to connect to other internet users, even strangers, all around the world.

_____ **U.** The transmission of data over phone lines opened up many opportunities and minimized our dependence on more traditional methods of communication.

Paragraph 5

When, or shortly after, Francis Scott Key wrote his poem "Defence of Fort McHenry," he knew he wanted to set it to the tune of "The Anacreon in Heaven," a popular British song at the time.

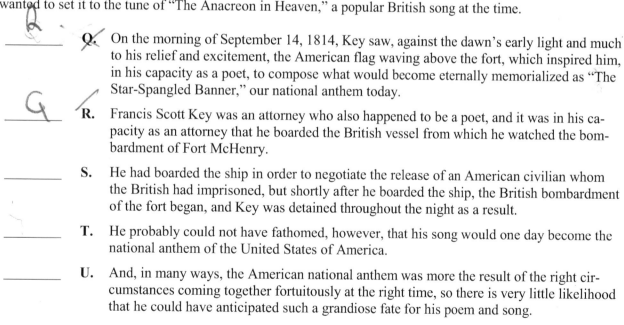

_____ **Q.** On the morning of September 14, 1814, Key saw, against the dawn's early light and much to his relief and excitement, the American flag waving above the fort, which inspired him, in his capacity as a poet, to compose what would become eternally memorialized as "The Star-Spangled Banner," our national anthem today.

_____ **R.** Francis Scott Key was an attorney who also happened to be a poet, and it was in his capacity as an attorney that he boarded the British vessel from which he watched the bombardment of Fort McHenry.

_____ **S.** He had boarded the ship in order to negotiate the release of an American civilian whom the British had imprisoned, but shortly after he boarded the ship, the British bombardment of the fort began, and Key was detained throughout the night as a result.

_____ **T.** He probably could not have fathomed, however, that his song would one day become the national anthem of the United States of America.

_____ **U.** And, in many ways, the American national anthem was more the result of the right circumstances coming together fortuitously at the right time, so there is very little likelihood that he could have anticipated such a grandiose fate for his poem and song.

CONTINUE ▶

LOGICAL REASONING
QUESTIONS 11-25

DIRECTIONS: For each question, read the information provided and select the **best** answer choice, based **only on the information given.** In other words, even if you know more about a particular set of facts than is provided, do not use outside facts to aid your decision-making process.

When dealing with logical reasoning questions, be on alert for certain placement or position and order words and phrases, such as **to the right of**, **above**, **before**, and **next to**. "The puppy is **between** the kitten and duckling," for instance, is not necessarily the same as "The puppy is **between and next to** the kitten and duckling"; one or more other objects may separate the puppy from the kitten or from the duckling.

---

11. Daniel's house is smaller than James's house. James's house and Richard's house are the same size. All the houses in Ashville are smaller than Richard's house.

    Based only on the information above, which of the following **must** be true?

    A. James's house cannot be in Ashville.
    B. At least one house in Ashville is bigger than Daniel's house.
    C. At least one house in Ashville is smaller than Daniel's house.
    D. Daniel's house is not in Ashville.
    E. Daniel's house is in Ashville.

12. The fastest swimmer on Team USA can eat four pizzas in one sitting. Ray can eat seven pizzas in one sitting.

    Based only on the information above, which of the following **must** be true?

    F. The fastest swimmer on Team USA is not the biggest swimmer on Team USA.
    G. Ray is not a swimmer on Team USA.
    H. The ability to eat pizzas in one sitting is related to swim speed.
    J. Ray is not the fastest swimmer on Team USA.
    K. Ray is a swimmer on Team USA.

13. Jamal has seven pets, but only three of them eat the same type of food. If he wants to keep two extra bags of each type of pet food around, in case of an emergency, how many extra bags of pet food must he keep in total?

    A. 5
    B. 7
    C. 8
    D. 10
    E. 14

14. If it is snowing heavily, I will not go to school. If it is a holiday, I will not go to school.

    Based only on the information above, which of the following **must** be true?

    F. If I did not go to school, then it is snowing heavily on a holiday.
    G. If I did go to school, then it is neither a holiday nor snowing heavily.
    H. If it is snowing lightly, then I may choose whether to go to school or not.
    J. It never snows where I live, so I always go to school.
    K. If it is not a holiday, then I will go to school.

CONTINUE ▶

15. Walking down a road, Kathy passed by six different automobile makes.

 1) The last automobile was a Fiat.
 2) The third automobile was a BMW.
 3) Kathy passed the Lexus after she passed both the Dodge and the Chevrolet but before she passed the Hyundai.
 4) The first automobile was not a Dodge.

What was the order in which she passed the automobiles, from first to last?

 A. Lexus, Hyundai, BMW, Dodge, Chevrolet, Fiat
 B. Hyundai, Lexus, BMW, Chevrolet, Dodge, Fiat
 C. Dodge, Lexus, BMW, Chevrolet, Hyundai, Fiat
 D. Fiat, Hyundai, Lexus, BMW, Dodge, Chevrolet
 E. Chevrolet, Dodge, BMW, Lexus, Hyundai, Fiat

16. Patrick, Timothy, Quentin, and Simon wanted to see who could throw a football the farthest.

 1) Timothy did not throw the football as far as Quentin did.
 2) Patrick threw the football farther than Simon did.

Based only on the information above, which of the following **must** be true?

 F. Patrick threw the football the farthest.
 G. If Patrick threw the ball the farthest, then Simon threw the ball the second farthest.
 H. If Quentin threw the ball the farthest, then Patrick threw the ball the second farthest.
 J. If Simon threw the ball farther than Timothy did, then either Patrick or Quentin threw the ball the farthest.
 K. Timothy threw the ball the least far.

17. Five students are sitting around at the edges of a table that is in the shape of a regular hexagon; they are facing the table.

 1) Alice is sitting across from Dylan.
 2) Dylan is not sitting next to the empty seat.
 3) Beth is sitting next to Frank and to his left.

If Frank is sitting next to Alice and to her left, what is the seating arrangement, starting with the empty seat and going to its **left**?

 A. (Empty)-Alice-Frank-Beth-Carter-Dylan
 B. (Empty)-Beth-Dylan-Carter-Frank-Alice
 C. (Empty)-Alice-Frank-Beth-Dylan-Carter
 D. (Empty)-Dylan-Beth-Carter-Alice-Frank
 E. (Empty)-Carter-Dylan-Beth-Frank-Alice

18. Mawsynram is the wettest place on Earth, receiving an average yearly rainfall of 474.4 inches. Atacama Desert receives an average yearly rainfall of fewer than 0.004 inches.

Based only on the information above, which of the following **must** be true?

 F. All places on Earth receive an average yearly rainfall of between 0.004 inches and 474.4 inches.
 G. On average, every place on Earth besides Mawsynram receives fewer than 474.4 inches of rain per year.
 H. Mawsynram receives more rain than Atacama Desert does every month.
 J. Atacama Desert is the driest desert on Earth.
 K. Every day, Mawsynram always receives more rainfall than any other place on Earth does in that same day.

CONTINUE ▶

19. A school held a field day for its students in which the students were divided into five teams, each team represented by a color. The last event of the day was a track and field event in which one representative from each team ran against the others. The colors were blue, red, yellow, orange, and green. There were no ties.

1) Justin was on the orange team.
2) Harold, who was on the green team, finished last.
3) Kylie finished after Irene and Lisa.
4) The red team finished first.
5) The yellow team finished before the blue team but after the orange team.

If Lisa finished after Irene, what place did Lisa finish in and what color team did she represent?

A. Lisa, on the orange team, finished first.
B. Lisa, on the blue team, finished second.
C. Lisa, on the yellow team, finished third.
D. Lisa, on the yellow team, finished last.
E. Cannot be determined from the information given.

20. From middle school to college, Clarisse played five years of tennis, seven years of field hockey, and five years of golf. She never played more than two sports in the same year, and she did not play the same sport multiple times in a year. Middle school is two years, high school is four years, and college is four years.

What is the **fewest** number of years Clarisse could have played sports during this time?

F. 8
G. 9
H. 10
J. 11
K. 12

21. Before lunch, four students in a class lined up single file to be dismissed.

1) Zack stood directly behind the student with the purple lunchbox.
2) Xavier stood behind Yolanda but ahead of Wendy.
3) Neither Wendy nor Yolanda has the purple lunchbox.
4) The student with the burgundy lunchbox stood behind the student with the lavender lunchbox but ahead of the student with the turquoise lunchbox.

Who stood third in line and what color lunch box did that student have?

A. Xavier, with a purple lunchbox.
B. Zack, with a burgundy lunchbox.
C. Xavier, with a turquoise lunchbox.
D. Wendy, with a turquoise lunchbox.
E. Cannot be determined from the information given.

22. Every wrestler at Lafonte High School also plays American football. Some soccer players also play American football. Paul participates as an athlete in exactly two of these sports.

Based only on the information above, which of the following **must** be true?

F. If Paul plays American football, he also wrestles.
G. Paul plays soccer and American football.
H. Paul does not play American football.
J. Paul wrestles and plays soccer.
K. If Paul plays soccer, then he does not also wrestle.

CONTINUE ▶

23. Neil is hunting for jobs and is constantly submitting applications and hearing back from them. Every prospective employer responds. If the prospective employer responds back to his job application by saying M, Neil always follows the procedure below:

1) After receiving response M, Neil immediately takes initiative A.
2) If initiative A fails, then Neil takes initiative X.
3) If either A or X succeeds, then Neil takes initiative K.
4) If X fails, then Neil applies procedure Y.
5) Any given initiative or procedure can only either succeed or fail.

After receiving a response of M from a prospective employer, Neil neither took initiative X nor applied procedure Y.

Based only on the information above, which of the following **must** be true?

A. Neil took initiatives A and K.
B. Neil took initiative K, which succeeded.
C. Neil can apply procedure Y before he takes initiative X.
D. If procedure Y fails, then Neil retries initiative A.
E. Cannot be determined from the information given.

Questions 24 and 25 refer to the following information.

In the code below, (1) each letter always represents the same word, (2) each word is represented by only one letter, and (3) in any given sentence, the letters may or may not be presented in the same order as the words.

"Diana	walked	to	the	mall."	means
K	W	C	Z	Y	

"Steph	walked	to	her	house."	means
Z	A	Y	M	H	

"Liam	walked	to	the	zoo."	means
Q	W	Y	Z	S	

"Carl	walked	to	his	house."	means
B	Y	M	P	Z	

24. Which letter represents the word "house"?

F. A
G. H
H. Y
J. M
K. Cannot be determined from the information given.

25. How many letters could be assigned to more than one word?

A. 7
B. 8
C. 9
D. 10
E. 11

CONTINUE ▶

READING

QUESTIONS 26-50

DIRECTIONS: Each passage below has five questions associated with it. After reading a passage, answer the questions, based **only on the information provided** by the passage; even if you have a deeper knowledge of the contents of the passage, do not base your answers on any outside knowledge.

On December 1, 1955, at approximately 6 p.m., Rosa Parks boarded a bus in downtown Montgomery, Alabama. She sat down in the first available row for black patrons, but when the
5 front rows, which were reserved for white passengers, filled up, she and several others were instructed to move to other seats to accommodate the incoming white passengers.

Rosa Parks obdurately refused to stand up, even
10 as the others consented and gave up their seats. When the bus driver threatened to call the police on her, Parks calmly replied that he may do so, but that she would not budge. Her refusal to move may have been innocuous enough—she
15 did not see why she had to move, and she was tired of giving in—but it did exacerbate the tension on the bus and led to her arrest.

Rosa Parks's arrest sparked a problem that required a delicate solution that would have to ad-
20 dress the wrong she suffered but maintain peace in the community. Three days later, on December 4, 1955, such a solution was proposed: all black men and women were to boycott the buses until they were treated courteously, black drivers
25 were hired, and seating in the middle rows of the buses was on a "first come, first serve" basis.

Meanwhile, the war against segregation was also being waged in the courts. And on November 13, 1956, 381 days after the arrest of Rosa
30 Parks, the black community won a monumental legal and civil rights victory when the Supreme Court of the United States upheld a prior federal district court's ruling that Alabama's segregation laws for buses were unconstitutional.

35 The Montgomery Bus Boycott in turn inspired other boycotts around the nation, forcing many Americans to reevaluate their moral positions as they realized the vital contributions the collective of the black community made to society. It
40 also provided the springboard for Martin Luther King, Jr. to vault into the national spotlight as a champion of nonviolent protest and reform.

Through the greatly enhanced civil rights equality we enjoy today, Rosa Parks's legacy lives on.

26.   What is the main idea of this passage?

    F.   There have been many cultural icons who have promoted civil rights.
    G.   The Montgomery Bus Boycott was necessary for civil rights movements.
    H.   Rosa Parks was tired of giving in to the injustices of segregation.
    J.   Rosa Parks is iconic for her actions and the legacy left by her actions.
    K.   Rosa Parks is the greatest civil rights activist of all time.

27.   What solution was proposed to address the problem that the arrest of Rosa Parks sparked?

    A.   a peaceful march on Montgomery
    B.   a civil protest
    C.   a riot near the Montgomery bus depots
    D.   a boycott of the city buses
    E.   a petition for equal treatment

CONTINUE ▶

28. What can be inferred about seating arrangements on buses in Montgomery, Alabama, at the time Rosa Parks was arrested?

    F. Every row of the buses was available to all of the patrons on a "first come, first serve" basis, until seats began filling up, at which point the white patrons were given priority seating to wherever they wanted to sit.

    G. The back rows of the buses were set off for black patrons, but when the buses became too full, the black patrons were asked to step off the bus to make room for newly boarding white patrons.

    H. The back rows of the buses were reserved exclusively for black patrons, and no other minorities were permitted to sit in the back.

    J. The front rows of the buses were reserved for white patrons, and if those seats filled up, newly boarding white patrons were given priority to at least some of the rows made available for the black patrons.

    K. Before the Montgomery Bus Boycott, the middle rows of the buses were made available to all patrons on a "first come, first serve" basis.

29. Which of the following can be inferred from the passage?

    A. Rosa Parks refused to give up her seat because she was physically tired.

    B. Rosa McCauley legally changed her last name to Parks to avoid unnecessary acts of discrimination against her.

    C. Without Rosa Parks, Martin Luther King, Jr. could never have risen to prominence.

    D. Before the boycott, black drivers were not hired to drive buses.

    E. If not for the boycott, the city's bus systems would have made a fortune.

30. Which of the following statements is best supported by the passage?

    F. The Supreme Court would have eventually deemed segregation to be unconstitutional, even without Rosa Parks or the Montgomery Bus Boycott.

    G. Rosa Parks's refusal to give up her seat set in motion the events that would ultimately lead to the Montgomery Bus Boycott.

    H. Martin Luther King, Jr. would have risen to the same level of prominence even without the Montgomery Bus Boycott.

    J. It took under a year since the arrest of Rosa Parks for the Supreme Court to declare segregation on buses unconstitutional.

    K. The bus driver did not have to call the police because they happened to be nearby.

CONTINUE ▶

In his 1945 classic, *Animal Farm*, George Orwell allegorically depicts the shortcomings of the ideologies of Socialism and, in particular, the corruptions that power brings with it.

5   *Animal Farm* opens with Old Major, the eldest and most venerated animal on Manor Farm, sharing a dream he had of the day that all animals would be free from the bonds of slavery forced upon them by man. It is not known when
10 this liberation will take place, only that it will. As such, Old Major instills in the animals of Manor Farm the sense of duty to prepare for rebellion.

The rebellion Old Major spoke of comes early
15 and spontaneously. (It is difficult to pinpoint the cause of the rebellion, but the most plausible explanations involve some combination of the animals' growing discontentment with their situation on Manor Farm and the increasing neglect-
20 fulness of Mr. Jones towards the animals. It didn't help that Mr. Jones whipped them on the fateful day of the rebellion.)

The rebellion is monumentally successful—Mr. Jones, his wife, and his hired hands are expelled,
25 and the animals rename Manor Farm to Animal Farm and adopt Animalism, the tenets of which are laid out in the Seven Commandments, which in turn are condensed to, "Four legs good, two legs bad!"

30 With Snowball and Napoleon at its helm, Animal Farm is a rousing success. With two leaders and no unequivocally correct way to operate the farm, however, a multitude of logistical issues arise, as Snowball and Napoleon disagree at
35 every turn. Frustrated by his inability to outwit Snowball in their debates, Napoleon resorts to militancy and exiles Snowball from Animal Farm by unleashing on Snowball a pack of vicious dogs he had trained in secret for years—
40 Squealer later convinces the other animals that Snowball had plotted pernicious treachery against Animal Farm all along, which is why Napoleon drove him out.

Once Snowball is gone, Napoleon's grip on Ani-
45 mal Farm tightens, while his apathy increases

and adherence to the Seven Commandments loosens. The other animals are instinctively troubled but lack the proper evidence to refute the illegitimacy of the pigs' actions. As time passes,
50 Napoleon and the pigs become increasingly human, as they embrace the decorum and behaviors of man—by the end, they are indistinguishable from the humans they once so reviled.

31. Which of the following best states the purpose of *Animal Farm*?

    A. to promote the humane treatment of animals

    B. to illustrate how, if left unchecked, animals may conquer the world

    C. to show that if you mistreat those who work for you, they will rebel

    D. to advise against oligarchies

    E. to depict that Socialism is not pragmatic in the long run because total power corrupts people

32. What does the passage imply about Animalism?

    F. Animalism teaches that humans should be imprisoned for committing atrocities against animals.

    G. Animalism teaches equality among animals equal and avoidance of humans and human institutions.

    H. Animalism is the ideal that all animals are equal, but some are more equal than others.

    J. Animalism is about the survival of the fittest.

    K. It says animals should oppress humans in the same way that humans have oppressed animals.

CONTINUE ▶

33. Which of the following is NOT a contributing factor to the rebellion?

   A. the pigs' desire to rule the world
   B. Mr. Jones's neglectfulness
   C. Mr. Jones's whipping of the animals
   D. the animals' discontentment with Manor Farm
   E. Old Major's dream

34. Which of the following can be inferred from the passage about Snowball's exile?

   F. The dogs that Napoleon used were trained by police officers.
   G. Snowball was forced out of Animal Farm because he had been planning to destroy it.
   H. Napoleon had been planning it for some time.
   J. The animals voted to remove Snowball, once they learned of his treachery.
   K. Snowball left Animal Farm because he wanted to spread Animalism to other farms in the area.

35. Which of the following can be inferred from the passage?

   A. Every animal on Animal Farm abides by the Seven Commandments to the very end.
   B. The Seven Commandments are based on the Christian Bible's Ten Commandments.
   C. The pigs alter the Seven Commandments whenever they find it convenient to do so, but the others cannot prove this.
   D. If the Seven Commandments hadn't been created, then the pigs wouldn't have been able to obtain absolute power.
   E. The Seven Commandments were passed down to the animals by Old Major himself.

CONTINUE ▶

In 2011, Navy Lieutenant Brad Snyder lost his sight after he stepped on and triggered an improvised explosive device. In 2012, the lieutenant won two gold medals and one silver medal in the
5 London 2012 Paralympic Games and set a record for the men's 100-meter freestyle swimming event in the process. In doing so, he proved to himself and to the world that, while the explosion may have taken away his sight, it could not
10 quash his desire to compete at the highest levels.

Others such as Brazil's Alan Oliveira and China's Cheng Huang also riveted the world with their performances in their respective events, similarly proving that tragedies, even
15 life-altering tragedies, could not subdue their indomitable human spirits. They are not alone. Thousands of others have also triumphed brilliantly against all odds, thus epitomizing the values of the Paralympics—courage, determination,
20 inspiration, and equality—even if only three medalists are selected for each event.

Since its official inception in 1960,[1] the Paralympic Games have hosted over 38,000 athletes from at least 160 countries, spreading and pro-
25 moting their vision of "enabl[ing] Paralympic athletes to achieve sporting excellence and inspire and excite the world." It seems the Games are well on their way to fulfilling their vision. The 2012 London Games saw 4,200 athletes,
30 more than tenfold of the 400 who took part in the 1960 Games. Additionally, the audience turnout and ticket sales for the London 2012 Games have reached unprecedented levels—2.7 million tickets were sold and beat out the ticket
35 sales for the 2008 Beijing Games by approximately 900,000.

The Paralympic Games will continue to gain international traction with potential participants, media outlets, and the general public, and the
40 global awareness of the Paralympics will continue to reach new heights, allowing for the values and vision of the Paralympic Games to be better perpetuated.

---

[1] In 1948, a Professor Guttmann organized the Stoke Mandeville Games, which grew into the Paralympic Games by 1960.

36. What was the author's main purpose for writing this passage?

   F. to summarize just how popular the Paralympic Games have gotten recently, particularly in 2012
   G. to provide a brief context of the Paralympic Games and to highlight their significance
   H. to assert that disabilities and handicaps should never hold you back from accomplishing your goals
   J. to promote the values of the Paralympic Games to the world
   K. to showcase three of the athletes of the Paralympics and show they embody the spirit of the Games

37. What is the author's tone in this passage?

   A. skeptical and belittling
   B. awestruck and fawning
   C. impatient and unbiased
   D. informative and reverent
   E. humorous and ignorant

38. The passage assumes which of the following about the future of the Paralympic Games?

   F. The 2016 Games will outsell the 2012 Games by 900,000.
   G. Everyone in the world will embrace the vision and values of the Paralympics.
   H. Every future Paralympic Games will outsell the London 2012 Games.
   J. Future Paralympic athletes will display even more courage and determination.
   K. Generally, the global significance of the Paralympic Games will increase in the future.

CONTINUE ▶

39. Which of the following is implied by the passage?

    A. The Beijing 2008 Games sold the second most number of tickets of any Paralympics Game.

    B. Lieutenant Snyder was the best athlete to ever compete in the Paralympic Games.

    C. No other participant in the history of the Paralympics has sustained an explosives injury.

    D. No other Paralympic Games have sold as many tickets as the London 2012 Games.

    E. Every athlete to take part in the Paralympic Games has been honorable and inspirational role models.

40. Which of the following is not a value of the Paralympic Games?

    F. excellence
    G. inspiration
    H. courage
    J. determination
    K. equality

CONTINUE ▶

Conceived of by Édouard René de Laboulaye in 1865 and designed by French sculptor Frédéric-Auguste Bartholdi, the Statue of Liberty Enlightening the World was a gift to the people of the

5   United States from the people of France. Although Lady Liberty now stands majestically as a universal symbol of freedom and democracy, there was a time during her construction in which her fate was uncertain.

10   Originally, the Statue of Liberty was intended to be a gift to commemorate the centennial of the American Declaration of Independence and to celebrate the longstanding friendship between the two nations. As such, the plan entailed the

15   Statue's completion by 1876 as a joint project, with France building the Statue and America providing the Statue's site and the pedestal on which it would eventually stand.

As the project progressed, however, funding is-
20   sues plagued the Statue's construction, requiring both nations to rely on various fundraising methods to raise the money needed. In America, the fundraising went more slowly, as various legislative setbacks for the funding hampered the

25   project. Finally, in 1884, the American Committee for the Statue of Liberty ran out of funds for the pedestal, prompting newspaper publisher Joseph Pulitzer to action. By exhorting the American people to take action in his newspaper *New*

30   *York World*, Pulitzer successfully solicited contributions from over 125,000 people, for a total of more than $100,000 in a mere six months— the money raised was more than enough to ensure the completion of the pedestal.

35   Financing for the pedestal was completed in August 1885, and the pedestal itself was completed in April 1886. By then, the Statue had already been completed in France and had already arrived in New York Harbor. Assembly of the

40   Statue of Liberty began immediately and took four months to complete. After it was assembled, it was dedicated on October 28, 1886, a full ten years after it was supposed to have been—a happy belated centennial gift that was

45   thankfully seen through to the end by the dedicated people of America and France.

41. Which of the following best tells what this passage is about?

  A. what the Statue of Liberty stands for and the importance of cooperation between two countries on large scale projects
  B. how the Statue of Liberty came to be and one of the primary hurdles faced in its construction
  C. the types of fundraising events France and America employed to raise the money needed to complete the Statue
  D. who Joseph Pulitzer is and how he provided assistance to Lady Liberty's construction
  E. the lack of proper planning in the construction of the Statue of Liberty

42. What can be inferred from the passage about the year in which the Declaration of Independence was adopted?

  F. 1765
  G. 1775
  H. 1776
  J. 1785
  K. 1786

CONTINUE ▶

43. What can be inferred from the passage about the assembly of the Statue in America?

    A. The Statue was completed in mid-October of 1886.
    B. The Statue could have been completed more quickly if the weather conditions had been better.
    C. If the pedestal had been completed by August 1885, the Statue could have been fully assembled within the same year, or by early 1886, at the latest.
    D. The Statue could have been assembled earlier if the pedestal had been completed earlier.
    E. The Statue was dedicated a few days after it was completely assembled.

44. What can be inferred from the passage about Pulitzer's fundraising effort?

    F. Pulitzer himself did not want to contribute, so he resorted to asking the public for contributions.
    G. Pulitzer probably began asking the public for contributions sometime around the February of 1885.
    H. No one donated over two dollars.
    J. The money was raised in large part thanks to the millionaires.
    K. Most of the people contributing were cheap and stingy.

45. Whom would the author probably credit the most for the successful completion of the Statue?

    A. Joseph Pulitzer
    B. *New York World*
    C. the people of France and America
    D. Frédéric-Auguste Bartholdi
    E. the American Committee for the Statue of Liberty

CONTINUE ▶

Over 300 million people worldwide suffer from asthma, making it a nontrivial, global issue. Asthma is a chronic inflammatory disease or disorder of the airways that carry air to and from
5 the lungs. When the airways come in contact with an asthma trigger, the inner walls of the airways become sore and swollen and fill up with mucous, leading to shortness of breath, coughing, and wheezing—an asthma attack is a sud-
10 den worsening of these symptoms, and if the asthma attack is severe enough, it may cause damage to the internal organs and even death.

It is not yet certain if there is a single, greater underlying cause for asthma; it is only certain
15 that different people have different triggers and that certain factors, such as genetics and environment, are linked to asthma—everything from respiratory viruses to allergens to pollution has been linked to asthma. And though it is not pos-
20 sible to take genetic preventive measures against asthma, it is possible, or at least more feasible, to reduce exposure to the environmental triggers that cause asthma. Thus, for instance, if pollution is a trigger, then during periods of heavy
25 pollution, it is advisable for asthmatics to stay indoors.

In particular, it is important to detect the triggers for and prevent asthma in children—over 6 million children in the United States alone suffer
30 from asthma—because their lungs are still in development, and early detection and prevention can ensure a more enjoyable childhood and healthier adulthood. Yet, a recent study may have uncovered another possible asthma trigger,
35 one that may not be as per se obvious, thus perhaps making the war against asthma more difficult.

In a study funded by the National Institute of Environmental Health Sciences, a division of the
40 National Institute of Health, Dr. Tiina Reponen and her team of researchers collected dust samples from 289 homes that had infants whose average age was 8 months. They found that, by age 7, 69 (24%) of these children had developed
45 asthma. The team analyzed 36 species of mold and found that three were most commonly asso-

ciated with asthma: *Aspergillus ochraceus*, *Aspergillus unguis* and *Penicillium variabile*. They also found that remediating homes with mold
50 problems improved children's asthma.

Many factors contribute to the development and onset of asthma, but vigilance can go a long way towards minimizing the impact asthma can have.

46. What is the author's main purpose for this passage?

    F. to discuss the most common molds that contribute to the development of asthma in children

    G. to encourage, when possible, preventive measures for those with asthma

    H. to provide readers with a clear, yet concise, definition of asthma

    J. to bring to light just how widespread of a problem asthma is

    K. to emphasize the need for better asthma testing procedures for children

47. What can be inferred from the passage about the importance of taking preventive measures against asthma in children?

    A. Children's lungs are more vulnerable to the long term effects of asthma.

    B. All molds cause children to develop asthma, but three types are severely harmful.

    C. Genetically preventive measures should be taken against asthma whenever possible, especially if the asthmatic is a child.

    D. Children with asthma grow up to be unhappy adults, so it is important to make sure preventive steps are taken.

    E. Asthma must be prevented in children before they turn 7, to prevent adult asthma.

CONTINUE ▶

48. Based on the passage, what can be inferred about how asthma causes shortness of breath and other breathing problems?

   F. The soreness experienced in the airways prevents asthmatics from breathing properly.

   G. When the airways become inflamed and filled with mucous, the size of the openings of the airways is reduced.

   H. The symptoms brought on by their triggers greatly restrict the body's ability to intake air.

   J. The mucous that fills up the airways completely blocks the passage of air into the lungs.

   K. Asthma always leads to critical damage to internal organs.

49. Based on the passage, which of the following statements would the author most likely agree with?

   A. Only three species of mold have any effect on the development of asthma in children.

   B. Home owners, particularly those with young children, should consider getting their homes checked for mold.

   C. Asthma is the leading cause of death amongst respiratory conditions, diseases, and illnesses.

   D. Asthma is a wholly hereditary chronic inflammatory disease or disorder of the airways.

   E. Asthmatics should always wear surgical masks to prevent any triggers from entering into their airways.

50. If an asthma trigger is not as obvious, why might combating asthma be more difficult?

   F. because there would be no way to prevent the asthmatic from exposure to the trigger

   G. because it is theoretically impossible to test an asthmatic for every possible trigger imaginable

   H. because the underlying cause of asthma is unknown, if such an underlying cause even exists

   J. because an asthmatic may not think to reduce exposure to the trigger

   K. because the trigger is not visible to the human eye, it becomes harder for an asthmatic to reduce his or her exposure to the trigger

CONTINUE ▶

PART 2 — MATH

Suggested Time — 60 Minutes
50 QUESTIONS

GENERAL INSTRUCTIONS

Solve each problem and select the correct answer from the choices given. If you need space to do your work, you may use the test pages or on paper provided to you. ***DO NOT DO YOUR WORK ON YOUR ANSWER SHEET.***

NOTES:

(1) Diagrams may not be drawn to scale. Do not assume information about a diagram, unless it is specifically stated by the problem or on this page or it can be reasoned from the given information.

(2) Assume that the diagrams exist in a single plane unless otherwise specified by the problem.

(3) Reduce each fraction answer to the lowest terms unless otherwise specified.

SYMBOLS, FORMULAS, AND REPRESENTATIONS

The following reference chart may be useful as you solve the problems. You may refer to this page during the test.

SYMBOLS	MEANING
$\neq$	is not equal to
$<$	is less than
$>$	is greater than
$\leq$	is less than or equal to
$\geq$	is greater than or equal to
$//$	is parallel to
$\perp$	is perpendicular to

REPRESENTATIONS

Angles are represented by

Right angles are represented by

FORMULAS:

Circle's circumference: $2\pi r$

Perimeter of a rectangle: $2l + 2w$

Total triangle interior angle measure: $180°$

Total quadrilateral interior angle measure: $360°$

AREAS:

Triangles: $\frac{1}{2}bh$

Parallelograms: bh

Trapezoids: $\frac{1}{2}(b_1 + b_2)h$

Circles: πr^2

CONTINUE ▶

MATHEMATICS PROBLEMS

QUESTIONS 51-100

DIRECTIONS: Answer or solve each question or problem. Once you have arrived at the correct answer or come up with a satisfactory answer choice, mark your answer sheet accordingly.

---

51. $5.6 \div \dfrac{7}{4} =$

    A. 9.8
    B. 6.8
    C. 6.2
    D. 3.8
    E. 3.2

52. Every year, Elkfield County hosts a middle school math competition. In order to qualify, however, students must score an average of 92 on 6 qualifying tests. If Betty scored 88, 91, 99, 86, and 92 on her first 5 tests, what score must she *at least* receive on her 6th test to qualify for the competition?

    F. 84
    G. 86
    H. 88
    J. 95
    K. 96

53. Jaime is 14 years old. 5 years ago, he was a third of his uncle's age then. How old is his uncle now?

    A. 19
    B. 27
    C. 29
    D. 32
    E. 33

54. If $14x - 7y - 4 = 45$, what is the value of y in terms of x?

    F. $2x - 7$
    G. $7 - 2x$
    H. $2x + 7$
    J. $7 - 7x$
    K. $7 + 7x$

55. Four purple curtains of the same length are tied together. Two red ones, each 7 feet in length, are tied to the purple curtains to make a total curtain length of 62 feet. How long is each purple curtain?

    A. 10 ft.
    B. 11 ft.
    C. 12 ft.
    D. 13 ft.
    E. 14 ft.

56. How much less than 3.1672 is the value obtained by rounding 3.1647 to the nearest hundredth?

    F. 0.0088
    G. 0.0072
    H. 0.0016
    J. 0.025
    K. 0.25

CONTINUE ▶

57. What are the prime factors of 1650?

A. 2, 3, 5, 11
B. 3, 5, 10, 11
C. 1, 2, 3, 5, 11
D. 2, 3, 5, 10, 11
E. 1, 2, 3, 5, 6, 10, 11

58. *S* is 25% of *T*, and *T* is 2% of 25. What is the value of *S*?

F. 2

G. 1

H. $\dfrac{1}{2}$

J. $\dfrac{1}{4}$

K. $\dfrac{1}{8}$

59. $4xy(5wz - 3u) =$

A. $9wxyz - 7uxy$
B. $20wxyz - 12uxy$
C. $9wxyz - 12uxy$
D. $20wxyz - 3u$
E. $8uwxyz$

60.   A, B, and C are integers.
A – B is an even integer.
B + C is an even integer.

Which of the following **must** be true?

F. A × C is odd
G. A × C is even
H. A + C is odd
J. A + C is even
K. A ÷ C is an integer

61. What is the difference between 700% of 7 and 7% of 70?

A. 0
B. 42.3
C. 44.1
D. 47.5
E. 49

62. When *n* + 7 is divided by 5, the remainder is 4. What is the remainder when *n* is divided by 5?

F. 0
G. 1
H. 2
J. 3
K. 4

63.

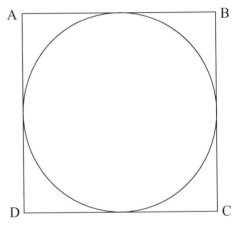

In the figure above, ABCD is a square with a circle inscribed within it. If a side of ABCD is 9 centimeters, what is the area of the circle in terms of π?

A. 81 sq cm
B. 18π sq cm
C. 20.25π sq cm
D. 40.5π sq cm
E. 81π sq cm

CONTINUE ▶

64. What is the value of $(w + z)(w - z)$ when $w = 6.25$ and $z = 3.75$?

    F. 25
    G. 12.5
    H. 10
    J. 5
    K. 2.5

65. For what value of m is $\dfrac{2(m-6)}{7} = 6$?

    A. 84
    B. 54
    C. 42
    D. 27
    E. 9.5

66.

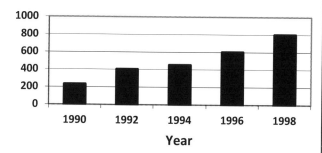

Population of Citysville in the Late 1990s (In Thousands)

Based on the graph above, in which year was Citysville's population approximately 300% of Citysville's population in 1990?

    F. 1990
    G. 1992
    H. 1994
    J. 1996
    K. 1998

67. If $z = 2w + 3$, what is the value of $4z - 5$ in terms of w?

    A. $3w + 8$
    B. $6w - 2$
    C. $6w + 12$
    D. $8w - 12$
    E. $8w + 7$

68. Ashley and Bobby handed out a total $4n - 5$ fliers. If Bobby handed out 5 more fliers than Ashley did, then in terms of n, how many fliers did Ashley hand out?

    F. n
    G. $2n - 5$
    H. $n - 10$
    J. $2n - 10$
    K. $4n + 5$

69. If A8,C49,FGH.KLM is a number where each letter represents a digit in the number, which letter will be in the thousandths place if the number is divided by 10,000?

    A. G
    B. H
    C. K
    D. L
    E. M

70. A cellist aims to practice 35 hours a week. If she practiced for 7 hours, 480 minutes, and 9 hours in 3 days, how many seconds must she practice for the rest of week to meet her goal?

    F. 11
    G. 660
    H. 6600
    J. 25600
    K. 39600

CONTINUE ▶

71. If the expression $\dfrac{6.8}{1.6K}$ is a positive integer, what is the smallest possible value of K?

   A. 1

   B. 10

   C. $\dfrac{17}{2}$

   D. $\dfrac{17}{4}$

   E. $\dfrac{4}{17}$

72. If $m > 0$ and $n < 0$, which expression **must** be negative?

   F. $n^2 - m$
   G. $n + m^2$
   H. $m^2 - n^2$
   J. $n - m^2$
   K. $m^2 + n^2$

73.

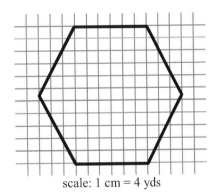

scale: 1 cm = 4 yds

About how much land is needed to create the full-sized hexagon above, if each square in the grid has a side length of 1 cm?

   A. 99 sq ft
   B. 156 sq ft
   C. 2372 sq ft
   D. 3564 sq ft
   E. 14256 sq ft

74. A jar contains 4 blue, 5 red, 9 orange, and 6 green beads. Kelly removed 3 beads, two of which were orange. If she removes one more randomly, what is the probability that it will not be orange?

   F. $\dfrac{1}{3}$

   G. $\dfrac{2}{3}$

   H. $\dfrac{1}{8}$

   J. $\dfrac{7}{8}$

   K. $\dfrac{1}{2}$

75. George is currently g years old, and Mike is currently m years old, where g and m are positive integer values. 8 years ago, Mike was one fourth as old as George was then. How old could Mike be now?

   A. 5
   B. 6
   C. 7
   D. 8
   E. 9

76. A botanist wants to build a garden to grow flowers. The garden is to be three-fourths as wide as it is long. If the garden is 24 feet long, then how much of his land will the botanist need to reserve?

   F. 576 sq yd
   G. 432 sq yd
   H. 108 sq yd
   J. 48 sq yd
   K. 24 sq yd

CONTINUE ▶

77.

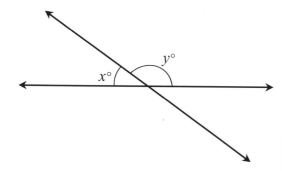

In the figure above, if the value of y is 1.5 times that of x, what is the value of $2y - x$?

A. 72
B. 108
C. 144
D. 180
E. 288

78. A thirteen-sided polygon has 4 sides each of m inches in length, 3 sides each of $m + 2$ inches in length, and 3 sides each of $2m - 3$ inches in length. The remaining three sides have lengths of 9 inches, 11 inches, and 15 inches. If the total perimeter is 97 inches, what is the value of m?

F. 1
G. 3
H. 5
J. 6
K. 8

79. If $x = \sqrt{6^2} + \sqrt{8^2}$ and $y = \sqrt{6^2 + 8^2}$, what is $x - y$?

A. 4
B. 6
C. 8
D. 10
E. 14

80. On a map, 1 centimeter represents 100 miles. How many square centimeters on the map represent 10 square miles?

F. 0.0001 sq cm
G. 0.001 sq cm
H. 0.01 sq cm
J. 0.1 sq cm
K. 1 sq cm

81.

What is the difference of the lengths of $\overline{OR}$ and $\overline{OP}$?

A. 4
B. 6
C. 10
D. 12
E. 16

82. 469 people attended a governor's speech at a park, which had bench seating for 540 people. If people file in and fill up each bench completely before beginning to occupy a new bench, and each bench seats 15 people, how many people occupy the last bench to be seated?

F. 1
G. 2
H. 4
J. 8
K. 15

CONTINUE ▶

83.

STATE PARK PATRONS

Day	1	2	3	4	5	6	7	8
# of Patrons	153	203	186	177	153	194	98	203

What was median number of patrons to the state park for the days shown above?

A. 125.5
B. 181.5
C. 190
D. 198.5
E. 203

84. There are 4,500 bees in an apiary. Of 75 bees collected for health screening, 35 are workers and 40 are drones. Which is the best estimate of the number of worker bees in the apiary?

F. 4,250
G. 3,200
H. 2,735
J. 2,400
K. 2,100

85.

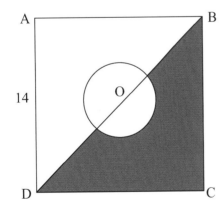

In the square ABCD, what is the area of the shaded region, if O is a circle in the middle of ABCD with a radius of 3 and AD = 14?

A. $49 - 6\pi$
B. $49 - 9\pi$
C. $98 - 2.5\pi$
D. $98 - 4.5\pi$
E. $98 - 6\pi$

86. There are 660 feet in one furlong, 8 furlongs in one mile, and 3 miles in one league. How many yards are in 2.5 leagues?

F. 24
G. 1760
H. 13,200
J. 15,840
K. 26,400

87. Jimmy ran $\dfrac{5}{13}$ as many laps as Steve did. If Steve ran 39 laps, and each lap is a quarter of a mile, how many miles did Jimmy run?

A. 3.75
B. 7.5
C. 15
D. 65
E. 39

88. Ash turned a years old today. Cal is 5 years younger than Ash. In terms of a, how old will Cal be in 14 years?

F. $a - 5$
G. $a + 5$
H. $a + 14$
J. $a - 9$
K. $a + 9$

89. Ty and Rob ordered three pies. Ty ate five-twelfths of a pie, and Rob ate three times as much as Ty did. What is the ratio of the amount of pie eaten to the amount remaining?

A. 5:4
B. 4:5
C. 2:3
D. 3:2
E. 1:4

CONTINUE ▶

90. In a popularity contest between two high school seniors, 3,500 of the school's student population of 4,000 voted. The winner received 60% of the votes cast, while the losing student received the remainder of the votes. If each student cast one vote only, what percent of the total student body voted for the losing student?

F. 20
G. 25
H. 30
J. 35
K. 40

91. If $\dfrac{5p - 2q}{8} = 4q$, what is the value of q in terms of p?

A. $\dfrac{5p}{34}$

B. $\dfrac{34p}{5}$

C. $\dfrac{5}{34p}$

D. $\dfrac{34}{5p}$

E. $\dfrac{17}{5p}$

92. $\{1, 2, 3, 4, \ldots, 200, 201, 202\}$

How many numbers in the set above are multiples of 3 but not also of 6?

F. 67
G. 66
H. 34
J. 33
K. 21

93. Lee bought a bag of 52 jelly beans. He counted 14 red, 12 green, and 8 purple jelly beans. The rest were pink. By random chance, he picked 6 green ones in a row and ate them. What is the probability that the next jelly bean he picks will be green?

A. $\left(\dfrac{1}{6}\right)^7$

B. $\dfrac{1}{6}$

C. $\dfrac{3}{23}$

D. $\dfrac{1}{9}$

E. $\dfrac{3}{13}$

94.

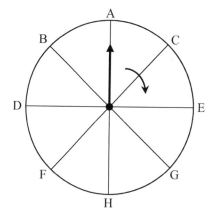

In the circle above, the arrow rotates at 6 revolutions per minute. If the arrow starts at A, how many seconds are needed for the arrow to point to F for the fifteenth time?

F. 180
G. 156.25
H. 150
J. 146.25
K. 140

CONTINUE ▶

95.

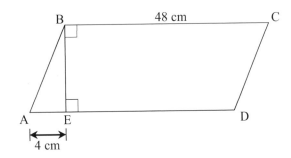

What is the area of triangle ABE if the perimeter of parallelogram ABCD is 106 centimeters?

A. 12 sq cm
B. 6 sq cm
C. 13 sq cm
D. 24 sq cm
E. 9 sq cm

96. If all of the dimensions of a block measuring 15 feet long, 18 inches wide, and 6 feet high are reduced by 50%, what would the block's compacted volume be?

F. 0.625 cu yd
G. 2.5 cu yd
H. 5 cu yd
J. 135 cu yd
K. 1620 cu yd

97. A tiger is tied to an interior corner of a steel cage by a $40\sqrt{2}$-foot rope. The cage measures 90 feet by 40 feet. How much area can the tiger access?

A. $400(\pi + 4)$ sq ft
B. $400(\pi + 2)$ sq ft
C. $400(\pi + 1)$ sq ft
D. $200(\pi + 6)$ sq ft
E. $800(\pi - 2)$ sq ft

98. If two of a square's opposite corners have coordinates of (0, 0) and (0, 5), how many square units are in the area of the square?

F. 5
G. 7.5
H. 10
J. 12.5
K. 25

99. Evaluate the expression

$$\frac{1}{4}\left[8\left(\frac{1-2}{2+3}\right)\left(\frac{3+2}{2-1}\right)\right]$$

A. -2
B. -1
C. 0
D. 1
E. 2

100.

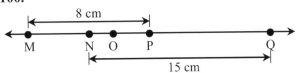

On the number line above, if OP = 2(NO) and MQ = 20, what is the length of $\overline{OQ}$?

F. 3
G. 4
H. 7.5
J. 10
K. 14

STOP. THIS IS THE END OF THE TEST. IF TIME PERMITS, YOU MAY REVIEW YOUR ANSWERS TO PARTS 1 AND 2 OF THE TEST.

SHSAT
TJHSST EDITION
TEST 2

PART 1 — VERBAL
Suggested Time — 60 Minutes
45 QUESTIONS

SCRAMBLED PARAGRAPHS
PARAGRAPHS 1-5

DIRECTIONS: The purpose of this section is to organize sentences into the best six-sentence paragraphs possible. For each paragraph, the first sentence is provided, but the remaining five are presented in random or no particular order. Re-order and organize these five sentences, if necessary, to create the **most** logical paragraph. Each paragraph is worth **two** points, whereas every other question type in this test is worth one. Partial credit will not be given.

Blanks have been provided to help you keep track of the position of each sentence in the paragraph. For instance, if you think a sentence follows the first, given sentence, write "2" in the blank next to it; write "3" next to the sentence that you believe follows "2"; and so on. When you believe you have arranged the sentences correctly, transfer your response to your answer sheet.

Paragraph 1

As one of the most abundant elements on Earth, iron would probably not qualify as a precious metal by most people's standards.

_____ Q. But if value were based on utility and necessity, iron would top, or at least come very close to topping, the list of expensive metals.

_____ R. Certainly, no one in his right mind would pay as much per unit weight for iron as he would for gold, platinum, or titanium.

_____ S. Ever since then, iron has become the most widely used metal element, making it arguably the most important—in fact, iron even serves essential life-sustenance functions in the majority of living organisms.

_____ T. Its usefulness was first truly discovered sometime after 2000 B.C.E., when the Hittites discovered that weapons forged from iron were harder, more durable, and sharper than those made of bronze, which was the prevailing metal used at the time.

_____ U. The Hittites guarded the secrets of iron forging for hundreds of years, but when their empire eventually collapsed, their secrets spread out to the rest of the world, thus ushering in the Iron Age.

CONTINUE ▶

Paragraph 2

On October 4, 1957, the Soviet Union not only made history but also altered the course of history by launching the first viable artificial satellite to orbit the Earth.

_____ **Q.** This proved beyond any reasonable doubt that the Soviet Union could attack the United States with ballistic missiles carrying nuclear warheads and added to the already escalating tensions of the Cold War, which they were embroiled in at the time.

_____ **R.** Perhaps the biggest impact of Sputnik I's launch was the deterioration of the confidence of the American public, who, up to that point, had firmly believed that the Soviet Union was a technologically inferior nation.

_____ **S.** It did not help the Americans' confidence that a modified SS-6 Sapwood intercontinental ballistic missile had served as the launch vehicle for Sputnik I.

_____ **T.** As a result of its denizens' growing unrest, the United States responded in kind to the Soviet Union with its own satellite, thus fueling even more competition and ultimately leading to many great scientific discoveries and technological innovations.

_____ **U.** The satellite, named Sputnik I, was small—it was approximately the size of a beach ball and weighed 183.9 pounds—but the significance of its launch was far from small.

Paragraph 3

The word _paper_ comes from the papyrus plant _Cyperous Papyrus_, from which the Ancient Egyptians fashioned the precursor to paper nearly 5,000 years ago.

_____ **Q.** In truth, archaeological records indicate that there were others who created paper before Ts'ai Lun did, but he is attributed with the invention of paper because his paper-making efforts were the first to be recorded.

_____ **R.** What the Egyptians made wasn't quite paper—it was more of a mat made from interwoven reeds or stalks made from the stem of papyrus plant.

_____ **S.** And even though some of the broader principles involved in the making of papyrus are also implemented in the making of paper, it wouldn't be another 3,000 years or so until paper was invented by Ts'ai Lun, a Chinese government official and scholar.

_____ **T.** This allowed the Egyptians to more easily pound the interlaced strips of papyrus plant flat, causing the strips to mesh together into a single thin sheet, which was in turn laid out in the sun to dry.

_____ **U.** But before they were crisscrossed to form the mat, the reeds were soaked in water and allowed to rot slightly.

CONTINUE ▶

Paragraph 4

Skin color does matter—in a biological sense, that is.

_____ **Q.** And, ultimately, what this all means is that darker skinned persons should be more cognizant about vitamin D_3 intake and lighter skinned persons should be more cautious about going into sun without sunblock or sunscreen.

_____ **R.** Melanin is able to help reduce photodamage by absorbing and scattering UVB radiation— there are three main types of ultraviolet radiation, of which UVB is one.

_____ **S.** But there is a tradeoff to being able to absorb more UVB radiation: with more melanin to compete against, 7-dehydrocholesterol becomes less able to absorb the UVB it needs to be converted to vitamin D_3.

_____ **T.** Studies have shown that lighter skin typically produces more vitamin D_3, which is essential to calcium absorption and immune system function, than darker skin does.

_____ **U.** Unfortunately, though, it is less effective at protecting against sun-induced damage because it does not contain as much melanin, the dark pigment that contributes to skin, hair, and iris color, as its darker counterpart does.

Paragraph 5

Many facts remain unknown about the life of the pirate Blackbeard, but one thing is certain: he was one of the most feared pirates from 1716 to 1718.

_____ **Q.** He outfitted his new ship with forty cannons, transforming the large slaver into one of the most powerful pirate ships to terrorize the American and Caribbean coasts.

_____ **R.** Before Edward Teach, as is believed to be Blackbeard's true name, became the infamous pirate of yore, he served briefly under Captain Benjamin Hornigold, who, after the War of the Spanish Success, had turned to piracy.

_____ **S.** And despite that many colonists put up with Teach and his pirates because it was often cheaper to buy the pirates' stolen goods than it was to import the goods from Europe, Teach's criminal reign didn't last a long time.

_____ **T.** Under the tutelage of Hornigold, Teach developed the skills he would need to eventually lead his own boat as a pirate captain, a French slave ship that he had stolen and renamed from *Le Concorde* to *Queen Anne's Revenge*.

_____ **U.** Blackbeard, as Teach had established himself, died in 1718, during a skirmish that ensued when Alexander Spotwood, the governor of Virginia, tried to have him captured.

CONTINUE ▶

LOGICAL REASONING
QUESTIONS 11-25

DIRECTIONS: For each question, read the information provided and select the **best** answer choice, based **only on the information given.** In other words, even if you know more about a particular set of facts than is provided, do not use outside facts to aid your decision-making process.

When dealing with logical reasoning questions, be on alert for certain placement or position and order words and phrases, such as **to the right of**, **above**, **before**, and **next to**. "The puppy is **between** the kitten and duckling," for instance, is not necessarily the same as "The puppy is **between and next to** the kitten and duckling"; one or more other objects may separate the puppy from the kitten or from the duckling.

11. Jorge plans his schedule for the upcoming week. He will study at least one subject, but not more than three, per day. He doesn't study any subject more than once a day.

    Jorge will study science four times, English two times, math four times, and history five times. What is the most number of days he can study three subjects in a day?

    A. 2
    B. 3
    C. 4
    D. 5
    E. 6

12. Every adult in Hentown is over two meters tall. Some adults in Hentown are farmers, and all Hentown farmers are adults. Some farmers are athletes.

    Based only on the information above, which of the following **must** be true?

    F. All farmers are good athletes.
    G. Some Hentown farmers are athletes.
    H. Every athlete in Hentown is a farmer.
    J. Children in Hentown are under two meters tall.
    K. All Hentown farmers are taller than two meters.

13. Bobby, the fastest student in his class, can run a mile in six minutes. When Teresa entered a mile race, she won first place.

    Based only on the information above, which of the following **must** be true?

    A. If Teresa is in Bobby's class, Teresa can run a mile in under six minutes.
    B. Teresa is not in Bobby's class.
    C. If Teresa is not in Bobby's class, Teresa can run a mile in under six minutes.
    D. Bobby did not enter the race.
    E. If Teresa is in Bobby's class, either Bobby did not race or Bobby ran the race in over six minutes.

14. A dance troupe wants to incorporate three square formations in its performance. The three squares will have side lengths of three, four, and five dancers, respectively. How many dancers are needed in total, if each dancer can belong to only one square?

    F. 12
    G. 22
    H. 24
    J. 36
    K. 48

CONTINUE ▶

15. Moe will not attend the fair if Jay does. Jay will attend the fair if Ann is able to get to Jay's house on time.

Based only on the information above, which of the following **must** be true?

A. If Jay does not attend the fair, Moe will.
B. Neither Jay nor Moe will attend the fair.
C. Moe will not attend the fair if Ann attends.
D. If Ann is able to get to Jay's house on time, Moe will not attend the fair.
E. Moe will attend the fair if Ann does not.

16. Five girls wanted to see who could blow the biggest bubble without it popping.

1) Zelma blew the third biggest bubble.
2) Wanda's bubble popped before Val's.
3) May's bubble popped right before Tara's.

Based only on the information above, which of the following **must** be true?

F. If Val's bubble was the smallest, then May's was the second biggest.
G. If Tara's bubble was second smallest, then Val's was the biggest.
H. Wanda's bubble was the biggest.
J. If May's bubble was second smallest, then Wanda's was the smallest.
K. Tara's bubble popped right before Val's.

17. Five students, Pat, Roger, Sasha, Trey, and Ursula, stood in line for a water slide.

1) Sasha was second in line.
2) Trey was immediately after Pat in line.

Based only on the information above, which of the following **must** be true?

A. If Ursula is third, then Pat is fourth.
B. Pat is first in line.
C. Roger is first in line.
D. If Roger is third, then Ursula is last.
E. Sasha is two places in line ahead of Trey.

18. Aimee does something cultural at least once a week, but she does not goes to the same type of event more than once in any given week. She likes to choose between an opera house, museum, book club, and sports event.

1) If she goes to the sports event, she will go to neither the museum nor the book club.
2) If she goes to the opera house, she will not go to the sports event.
3) If she goes to the book club, then she will not go to the museum.

If Aimee goes to two cultural events in a week, which of the following **must** be true?

F. Aimee goes to the opera house.
G. Aimee goes to the museum.
H. Aimee goes to the sports event.
J. Aimee goes to the book club.
K. Aimee cannot go to two events in a week.

19. A student is organizing five of his books, whose covers are all different colors, from left to right.

1) The red book is second from the left, and two books separate the red book from the yellow book.
2) The econ book is in the leftmost position.
3) The math book is immediately to the left of the psych book, which has a blue cover.
4) The blue book is placed to the left of the green book.

Which position is the orange book in?

A. Rightmost
B. Second from the right
C. Center
D. Second from the left
E. Leftmost

CONTINUE ▶

55

20. India is the world's second most populous nation, with more than 1.2 billion people. The Pitcairn Islands has a population of 48.

Based only on the information above, which of the following **must** be true?

    F. If China's population is 1.3 billion, then China is the most populous nation.

    G. If the Cocos Islands has a population of 40, then it is the least populous nation.

    H. If Vietnam's population is 91.5 million, and Thailand's population is 67 million, then Thailand is at best the fourth most populous nation.

    J. The Pitcairn Islands is the least populous nation.

    K. If India's population is fewer than 1.3 billion, then China is the most populous nation.

21. On her way to work, Rena passes six different flowers.

    1) She passes the daisy first.

    2) She passes the tulip before she passes the lily, which she passes before the rose.

    3) She passes the carum immediately before she passes the violet.

Based only on the information above, which of the following **must** be true?

    A. The tulip is second.

    B. The lily is either third or fifth.

    C. The rose is last.

    D. Rena passes the violet before passing the rose.

    E. The carum is either third, fourth, or fifth.

22. Dolores, Evan, Finny, Georgette, and Herschel all work at a zoo. Each was to propose a specific animal to add to the zoo. They presented their proposals one at a time.

    1) The nightingale was proposed second.

    2) Herschel proposed the crocodile before Finny proposed the aardvark.

    3) Dolores made her proposal immediately after Georgette did.

    4) The swordfish was presented before the aardvark.

    5) The iguana was presented last.

Based only on the information above, which of the following **must** be true?

    F. The crocodile was proposed third.

    G. The swordfish was proposed third.

    H. Dolores proposed the iguana last.

    J. Georgette proposed the iguana last.

    K. Finny proposed the aardvark fourth.

23. The smallest member of the Tigers scores four goals every game, making him, on average, the team's leading scorer. During one game in particular, Bret scored five goals.

Based only on the information above, which of the following **must** be true?

    A. Bret is the smallest player of the Tigers.

    B. Smaller players score more goals per game, on average.

    C. Bret is not a player on the Tigers.

    D. If Bret is a player on the Tigers, he is not the smallest player.

    E. If Bret is not a player on the Tigers, he is the smallest player on his team.

CONTINUE ▶

Questions 24 and 25 refer to the following information.

In the code below, (1) each letter always represents the same word, (2) each word is represented by only one letter, and (3) in any given sentence, the position of a letter is **never** the same as that of the word it represents.

H	P	S	L	B	means
"Fred	drinks	milk	and	water."	

K	Y	P	T	J	means
"Clara	eats	pizza	and	lasagna."	

L	J	R	A	P	means
"Louis	likes	pizza	and	water."	

A	P	X	Y	Q	means
"Mitch	likes	lasa-gna	and	fries."	

24. Which letter represents the word "Louis"?

    F. R
    G. A
    H. L
    J. J
    K. Cannot be determined from the information given.

25. Which letter stands for "eats"?

    A. T
    B. J
    C. Y
    D. K
    E. Cannot be determined from the information given.

CONTINUE ▶

READING

QUESTIONS 26-50

DIRECTIONS: Each passage below has five questions associated with it. After reading a passage, answer the questions, based **only on the information provided** by the passage; even if you have a deeper knowledge of the contents of the passage, do not base your answers on any outside knowledge.

The Civil War ships USS *Monitor* and *Merrimack* are notable for their involvement in the Battle of Hampton Roads, the naval battle that would feature, for the first time in the history of
5 the world, two ironclads fighting against one another for naval supremacy.

On March 9, 1862, a day after handily defeating USS *Congress* and *Cumberland* and killing over 240 of their crew in the process, CSS *Virginia*,
10 which had previously served as the frigate USS *Merrimack*, was ready to strike again. This time, it had in its sights the grounded steam frigate *Minnesota* and other warships. A victory here would greatly loosen, if not almost completely
15 divest, the lower Chesapeake Bay region of the Union's hold—the Union fleet had established a blockade that prevented international trade for some of Virginia's key cities, including Richmond and Norfolk. *Virginia* was thus strategi-
20 cally important to the Confederacy's military plans.

What the crewmembers of *Virginia* and the rest of the Confederacy did not expect, however, was the arrival of the Union's own ironclad to aid the
25 defense of the immobile *Minnesota*. Still, *Monitor*'s arrival did not deter *Virginia* from launching its assault. Both boats exchanged heavy fire. *Virginia*'s smokestack was blown away, and Lieutenant John L. Worden, *Monitor*'s com-
30 manding officer, was blinded when *Virginia* concentrated its attack on *Monitor*'s pilothouse, but the heavy iron plating covering the sides of the ships prevented each from sustaining any crippling damages.

35 In the end, neither ironclad was able to score a decisive victory. By the time *Monitor* was able

to withdraw to relieve Lieutenant Worden and redeploy to face *Virginia* once again, all the while valiantly protecting *Minnesota*, the Con-
40 federate ship had already set sail for its naval base in Norfolk. There would be no rematch that would allow for the determination of a true champion.

And though the Battle of Hampton Roads was
45 not the first time an ironclad was used for combat purposes, it did underscore one key point: the end of the era of wooden naval vessels was nigh.

26. What is the main purpose of this passage?

    F. to argue that *Monitor* and *Virginia* were the strongest ships in the world at the time.

    G. to provide a historical context for two of the Civil War's most significant warships

    H. to illustrate the extent of the ironclads' power

    J. to discuss the underlying reasons behind the Battle of Hampton Roads

    K. to suggest that the Confederacy lost the Civil War because *Virginia* could not defeat *Monitor*.

CONTINUE ▶

27. Which of the following can be inferred from the passage?

    A. The ironclads were invincible to damage by wooden ships.
    B. Virginia was the only Confederate state that could engage in international trade.
    C. The Battle of Hampton Roads claimed more lives than any other naval battle of the Civil War did.
    D. *Virginia* had been dispatched in order to break through the Union's blockade of the Chesapeake.
    E. The ironclads were so evenly matched that it was impossible for one to decisively prevail over the other.

28. What question is left unanswered by the passage?

    F. Whom or what did *Monitor* come to protect?
    G. What was CSS Virginia's previous name, if any?
    H. Who was one of the commanding officers of *Monitor*?
    J. Why did *Virginia* sail away instead of trying to finish the battle with *Monitor*?
    K. On what date did CSS *Virginia* defeat *Congress* and *Cumberland*?

29. Which of the following would the author most likely agree with?

    A. Wooden warships were terminated immediately after the Civil War was over.
    B. Virginia's smokestack was not reinforced with heavy iron plating.
    C. Without the arrival of *Monitor*, the Union's blockade would have been significantly weakened, if not broken through.
    D. If *Monitor* did not have to focus on protecting *Minnesota*, it would have easily defeated *Virginia*.
    E. *Virginia* sailed away before *Monitor* redeployed because it knew it would lose.

30. Which of the following cities or places does the passage identify as the location of the Confederate naval base from which *Virginia* set sail?

    F. Norfolk
    G. Richmond
    H. Chesapeake Bay
    J. Hampton Roads
    K. It cannot be determined from the information given.

CONTINUE ▶

In January of 1692, Elizabeth Parris and Abigail Williams, ages 9 and 11, respectively, began to act as if they were possessed by some demonic spirit. They screamed, threw objects, contorted
5 their bodies abnormally, and uttered peculiar sounds. Soon thereafter, Ann Putnam, age 11, experienced similar outbursts. Then on February 29, 1692, three women were implicated in the bewitching of those girls, marking the beginning
10 of the dark period in history known as the Salem witch trials. But is it possible that a common food item was the driving cause of it all?

In the April 2, 1976, edition of *Science*, Linnda R. Caporael proposed that the fungus ergot
15 (*Claviceps purpurea*) may have been the culprit behind the witch hunt because of its toxicity to animals, including humans. Considering ergot was so commonplace that people thought it was a part of the grains on which it grew—ergot has
20 an affinity for rye, which was Salem Village's staple grain in the summer months—Caporael's hypothesis seems plausible. It would not remain unchallenged.

On Christmas Eve of the same year, *Science*
25 published another article coauthored by Nicholas P. Spanos and Jack Gottlieb that refuted Caporael's hypothesis as unlikely, by exposing potential holes in her argument. It begins by first explaining that there are two broad categories of
30 effects caused by ergot: gangrenous and convulsive; it is the latter that would have afflicted the Salem girls, had they been afflicted at all. And because convulsive ergotism occurs almost exclusively in locales where people suffer from se-
35 vere vitamin A deficiencies, Salem Village can be effectively ruled out. Ergot poisoning in people with sufficient vitamin A, on the other hand, leads to gangrenous ergotism, not convulsive ergotism. This is damning to Caporael's case,
40 Spanos and Gottlieb argue, because there were no reported incidents of even gangrenous ergotism, indicating that ergot had not been a factor at all.

We may never know who was correct—it was
45 either ergot or it wasn't that caused the girls to have fits—but the researchers' publications have certainly given us much to think about.

31. What is the main purpose of this passage?

   A. to demonstrate how simple it is to disprove another's argument or thesis
   B. to introduce a hypothesis that was offered to explain a historical phenomenon and a refutation against the hypothesis
   C. to prove that the outbursts that contributed to the start of the Salem witch trials were caused by a food item
   D. to promote greater awareness for the types of food that are eaten
   E. to use a historical example to advise against rashly jumping to conclusions

32. According to the passage, what can be inferred about why people voluntarily ate ergot?

   F. They knew about ergot's toxicity.
   G. They believed ergot to be a natural part of the grains they ate and, therefore, safe.
   H. They were convinced that ergot was killed during the winter time by the cold, so it did not matter if they ate ergot or not.
   J. They believed that ergot only grew on rye during the summertime.
   K. They did not have the proper means by which to clean ergot off the grains that they grew and harvested.

CONTINUE ▶

33. Which of the following, if true, would most greatly weaken Spanos and Gottlieb's hypothesis?

   A. Gangrenous ergotism afflicted many New Englanders, especially inhabitants of Salem Village.
   B. Diseases and illnesses were well documented by the doctors of Salem Village.
   C. Gangrenous ergotism only afflicted a handful of New Englanders.
   D. Gangrenous ergotism results in embarrassing symptoms, so incidents of it were never truthfully recorded in Salem.
   E. The girls who were apparently bewitched had an aversion to foods that were good sources of vitamin A.

34. Which was not among the behaviors exhibited by the three girls of Salem Village?

   F. screaming
   G. bodily contorting
   H. uttering strange sounds
   J. throwing objects
   K. frothing at the mouth

35. Which of the following can be inferred from the passage?

   A. Ingesting toxic substances can lead to abnormal behavioral patterns.
   B. The effects of ergot can last months, which explains how a summer crop affected the three girls in January.
   C. Vitamin A helps protect against ergotism.
   D. Exposure to toxic substances typically results in death.
   E. Salem Village did not have proper access to foods containing sufficient amounts of vitamin A.

CONTINUE ▶

A spotted hyena matriarch looks up from her feast, the fur around her mouth sanguine with the blood of her prey. She is alert to the turmoil erupting around her and finds herself faced with
5   a quandary: to eat or not to eat? Her hesitation lasts but a fleeting moment—a male African lion's strong jaws snap at her hindquarters, just barely missing their target; she is ravenous but not suicidal.

10   The dry season in Africa is difficult for all animals, predators and prey alike. The paucity of readily available water and an abundance of sun make for brutal living conditions, in which energy preservation is of paramount importance. It
15   is no wonder that the hyena is more reluctant to relinquish its fresh prey and the lion more eager to usurp the hyena's kill—every animal does what it needs to survive in these adverse conditions.

20   Even the lion, which is indisputably an apex predator, having been known to hunt adult elephants and hippopotamuses, is not above scavenging and pilfering the prey of other predators, and for good reason. The lion's heart makes up a
25   very small percentage of the lion's bodyweight (approximately half a percent). As a result, the lion can only sprint in short bursts. Because much energy is needed to sustain top speeds, it is often more sensible to "take the easy way
30   out." Hyenas, by contrast, hunt up to 95% of their food. Is, then, the king of beasts more accurately the king of thieves?

For millennia, from Aesop's *Lion and the Mouse* to Walt Disney's rendition of *Lion King*, the lion
35   has starred in many works of literature, media, and art, most often as a symbol of regality, strength, ferocity, and bravery. The hyena, on the other hand, has often been vilified, cast as everything from a witches' mount to a symbol of
40   immorality and the antithesis of virtue, including cowardice, stupidity, and greed. It is apparent we ascribe different sentiments to lions than we do to hyenas; it is not as apparent why we do.

Neither species is driven by the human concepts
45   of morality and virtue—there is no right and wrong in the animal kingdom, just survival—but

we often unfairly judge them and other animals as if they should adhere to our code of ethics.

36. What was the main idea of this passage?

F. Lions are just as evil as hyenas are.
G. The dry season in Africa brings out the worst in animals because they are forced to commit atrocities in order to survive.
H. It is at least somewhat unfair to pass judgment on animals, since they are only doing what they must to survive.
J. Animals have been the subjects of moral lessons and stories for thousands of years.
K. The male African lion is considered by many as the king of beasts, but it should be more appropriately labeled the king of thieves.

37. Which of the following can be inferred from the passage?

A. If lions had larger hearts, then they would hunt up to 95% of their food.
B. If lions had larger hearts, they would hunt elephants and hippopotamuses more often.
C. Humans are capable of outrunning lions in a marathon race.
D. If lions were not around, then hyenas would scavenge 95% of their food.
E. Heart size is a contributing factor to how long an animal can sustain its top speed.

38. Which of the following was not listed as a trait that the lion is representative of?

F. strength
G. regality
H. bravery
J. humility
K. ferocity

CONTINUE ▶

39. Which statement would the author most likely agree with?

    A. It is obvious why we ascribe different emotions to different animals.
    B. Lions are unquestionably top predators.
    C. Animals should adhere to our code of human morality and ethics.
    D. Non-human creatures are incapable of experiencing any sort of "human" emotion, such as sadness, happiness, and anger.
    E. Hyenas are extremely popular in some countries and cultures but much reviled in others.

40. According to the passage, which of the following contributes to the brutal conditions of the dry season in Africa?

    F. a shortage of both water and sun
    G. sweltering heat and a lack of prey
    H. the inability of predators to run at top speeds for very long
    J. too much sun and not enough water
    K. hunters and poachers killing off endangered animals

CONTINUE ▶

Situated in present-day Clark County, Las Vegas is, in its own right and in more ways than one, an oasis in a vast desert. The Las Vegas area was not, however, always so arid. Rafael Rivera, a
5 scout for a Mexican trading caravan led by Antonio Armijo in 1829, was the first person of European descent to discover the Las Vegas Valley region. He found extensive meadows that were supported by artesian wells in the area, which is
10 how Las Vegas got its name—Las Vegas is Spanish for "The Meadows."

As part of the concessions made by Mexico after the Mexican-American War, which ended on February 2, 1848, with the signing of the Treaty
15 of Guadalupe Hidalgo, the United States obtained a massive territory from Mexico now known as the Mexican Cession. This victory prize included California, Nevada, Utah, and parts of other states. And in the years following
20 this acquisition, Las Vegas would become a focal point for travelers, religious groups, and railroad companies because of its geographically strategic location, relative to other important cities.

25 For the Mormons, Las Vegas was a strategic location to build a fort because it was halfway between Salt Lake City and Los Angeles. Thus, in the spring of 1855, Brigham Young, the president of the Mormon Church at the time and the
30 founder of Salt Lake City, commissioned 30 Mormon missionaries led by William Bringhurst to set out to convert the Paiute Indians to Mormonism. Within two years, however, Young recalled his missionaries because of a power strug-
35 gle that broke out between Bringhurst and Nathaniel Jones, another one of the missionaries.

The next 50 years or so would see Las Vegas undergoing somewhat of an identity crisis. From its origins as a missionary post, it would first be-
40 come agricultural farmland and then later a railroad town. And despite its geographical significance, Las Vegas wasn't officially founded as a city until May 15, 1905. Moreover, it wasn't until after 1931, when gambling was legalized, that
45 Las Vegas gradually underwent the metamorphosis from city to Sin City, or "Entertainment Capital of the World."

41. Which of the following best tells what this passage is about?

A. how Las Vegas got its name
B. the irony that Las Vegas, now often referred to as Sin City, began in part as a religious establishment
C. the historical origins of Las Vegas
D. that the Mormons established a fort in Las Vegas because of the convenience of the area's geographical location
E. the evolution of Las Vegas from a Mormon settlement into a railroad town

42. What can be inferred from the passage about the Mexican-American War?

F. Las Vegas would become the most important city in the territory that the United States acquired from Mexico.
G. The Mexican Cession was what Mexico had to yield to the United States for losing the war.
H. Neither side won or lost, but they agreed to trade property as a gesture of friendship.
J. The Mexican Cession was the biggest land acquisition that the United States has ever made.
K. The treaty was drawn up by a man named Guadalupe Hidalgo.

CONTINUE ▶

43. Why did the Mormons abandon the fort that they built in the Las Vegas Valley?

    A. Nathaniel Jones did not agree with the way William Bringhurst was working the other missionaries like slaves, so a power struggle broke out.
    B. Two years was the original length of time that the Mormons had planned to stay.
    C. Brigham Young needed more help running Salt Lake City, the city he founded.
    D. Not enough Paiute Indians were converting to Mormonism.
    E. A dispute over the issue of control broke out between two of the missionaries that were sent there.

44. Which is not among the different types of purpose Las Vegas served over the years?

    F. industrial
    G. religious
    H. transit
    J. agricultural
    K. entertainment

45. According to the passage, what event marked the beginning of the perception people today have of Las Vegas?

    A. the discovery of Las Vegas Valley by Antonio Armijo in 1829
    B. the end of the Mexican-American War in 1848
    C. the establishment of the Mormon fort in 1855
    D. Las Vegas's founding as a city in 1905
    E. the legalization of gambling in 1931

CONTINUE ▶

Sometimes, it takes the sacrifice of one to pre-serve the lives of many. That's what happened in the case of United States Air Force (USAF) pilot Major Rudolf Anderson, Jr., whose plane was
5 shot down over Cuban airspace on October 27, 1962; his death may have averted a potential nu-clear war and global crisis.

Over the summer, the Soviet Union had drasti-cally increased its shipments of equipment and
10 personnel to Cuba. Nikita Khrushchev, the Premier of the Soviet Union, denied any military activity, but President Kennedy nonetheless au-thorized "Operation Brass Knob," a series of missions of high-altitude, Lockheed-made U-2
15 reconnaissance airplanes to be flown over the is-land nation. Thus, on October 14, 1962, Major Anderson flew over Cuba and successfully brought back photographic proof that the Soviets were arming it with nuclear weapons.

20 His discoveries also led to the unfortunate esca-lation of tensions that had already been running high. On October 22, President Kennedy pub-licly announced plans to quarantine Cuba from receiving offensive military equipment and to
25 heighten military alertness in the region. War loomed imminently on the horizon. So when Anderson was killed by the shrapnel of an ex-ploding surface-to-air missile (SAM) during yet another mission, war was all but certain.

30 When word of the shootdown reached the White House Cabinet Room, Kennedy was overwhelm-ingly urged to launch airstrikes against Cuba's air defense systems. The President chose not to, suspecting Khrushchev would not have author-
35 ized an order to shoot down an unarmed recon-naissance aircraft, given the tenuousness of the situation. He was correct. With the commanding general unavailable, Lieutenant General Stepan Grechko had given the launch order himself, de-
40 spite that the general was the only one author-ized to do so.

Major Rudolf Anderson, Jr. was the only casu-alty of the Cold War. For his courage and brav-ery, he was posthumously awarded the first ever
45 Air Force Cross, the service's highest distinction after the Medal of Honor, among other awards,

including the Purple Heart. His death was a can-did reminder of just how perilously close the Cold War had brought the world to war.

46. What is the main idea of this passage?

F. Major Anderson was a hero and there-fore properly awarded the medals he de-served.

G. If Lieutenant General Stepan Grechko had not authorized, without proper au-thorization, the shooting down of Major Anderson's aircraft, the Cold War would have escalated into actual nuclear conflict.

H. With Cold War tensions at an all-time high, an airman's heroic service and un-timely death reminded the world why peace was important.

J. Lives need to be sacrificed in order for world peace to be possible.

K. Courage and duty in the line of military service will be rewarded.

47. What was the purpose of Operation Brass Knob, as is implied by the passage?

A. to ease tensions between Cuba, the So-viet Union, and the United States

B. to reduce the number of casualties of the Cold War

C. to help the United States determine how to best quarantine Cuba from receiving Soviet Union shipments

D. to take aerial photographs to monitor the nuclear weaponization of Cuba

E. to fly high-altitude, Lockheed-made U-2 reconnaissance planes over Cuba in or-der to assess the planes' effectiveness

CONTINUE ▶

48. Why did President Kennedy refrain from launching a counterattack against the Soviet Union, despite being urged to do so?

   F. He knew that a nuclear war would be an extremely expensive ordeal that could potentially send the nation into another depression, and he did not want that.

   G. His advisors had been frequently wrong in the past, so he chose to ignore their advice.

   H. He wanted to avoid war at all costs, even if the Soviet leader had authorized the attack against Major Anderson.

   J. He did not feel that retaliation was worth the life of one American airman.

   K. He did not believe that Nikita Khrushchev would have ordered an attack against an unarmed reconnaissance aircraft.

49. According to the passage. what was the cause of Major Anderson's death?

   A. a direct hit from a surface-to-air missile

   B. a malfunction on his plane that prevented him from taking evasive maneuvers

   C. shrapnel from an exploding missile

   D. the inability of his plane's radar to detect incoming missiles

   E. his insistence that he fly a reconnaissance mission that particular day, even though his superiors did not want him to

50. Why was it special that Major Anderson was awarded the Air Force Cross?

   F. The Air Force Cross is even more prestigious than the Purple Heart.

   G. The Air Force Cross is the second highest medal an airman can earn, and Major Anderson was its first recipient.

   H. The Air Force Cross is the highest medal that an airman can earn, and Major Anderson deserved one for his heroism.

   J. The Air Force Cross was created specifically because of the extraordinary heroism Major Anderson displayed.

   K. The Air Force Cross is the highest medal that an airman can earn, and no one deserved it more than Major Anderson did, particularly considering he was the only casualty of the Cold War.

CONTINUE ▶

PART 2 — MATH

Suggested Time — 60 Minutes
50 QUESTIONS

GENERAL INSTRUCTIONS

Solve each problem and select the correct answer from the choices given. If you need space to do your work, you may use the test pages or on paper provided to you. ***DO NOT DO YOUR WORK ON YOUR ANSWER SHEET.***

IMPORTANT NOTES:
  (1) Diagrams may not be drawn to scale. Do not assume information about a diagram, unless it is specifically stated by the problem or on this page or it can be reasoned from the given information.
  (2) Assume that the diagrams exist in a single plane unless otherwise specified by the problem.
  (3) Reduce each fraction answer to the lowest terms unless otherwise specified.

SYMBOLS, FORMULAS, AND REPRESENTATIONS

The following reference chart may be useful as you solve the problems. You may refer to this page during the test.

SYMBOLS	MEANING
$\neq$	is not equal to
$<$	is less than
$>$	is greater than
$\leq$	is less than or equal to
$\geq$	is greater than or equal to
$//$	is parallel to
$\perp$	is perpendicular to

REPRESENTATIONS

Angles are represented by

Right angles are represented by

FORMULAS:

Circle's circumference: $2\pi r$

Perimeter of a rectangle: $2l + 2w$

Total triangle interior angle measure: $180°$

Total quadrilateral interior angle measure: $360°$

AREAS:

Triangles: $\frac{1}{2}bh$

Parallelograms: bh

Trapezoids: $\frac{1}{2}(b_1 + b_2)h$

Circles: πr^2

CONTINUE ▶

MATHEMATICS PROBLEMS

QUESTIONS 51-100

DIRECTIONS: Answer or solve each question or problem. Once you have arrived at the correct answer or come up with a satisfactory answer choice, mark your answer sheet accordingly.

---

51. If x is a positive integer and y is a negative integer, which of the following **must** be true?

   A. $x + y \geq 0$
   B. $y - x > 0$
   C. $y^2 \leq x^2$
   D. $(x - y)^2 = x^2 - y^2$
   E. $x - y > 0$

---

52. If V is 20% of W, and W is 18% of X, what percent of X is V?

   F. 38
   G. 28.2
   H. 10.4
   J. 3.6
   K. 2

---

53. If $4(3x - 5) = 2(y + 3)$, what is the value of y in terms of x?

   A. $3.5x - 7.5$
   B. $6x - 13$
   C. $7x - 13$
   D. $9x + 17$
   E. $12x - 23$

---

54. If a prime number is squared, how many factors does the resultant number have?

   F. 1
   G. 2
   H. 3
   J. 4
   K. It depends on the prime number being squared.

---

55. $7.8 \div \dfrac{13}{2} \times 8 =$

   A. 2.4
   B. 3.8
   C. 9.6
   D. 69
   E. 405.6

---

56. Reggie is 13 years older than his cousin Ramon. In 9 years from now, Reggie will be two times older than Ramon will be then. How old is Ramon now?

   F. 2
   G. 4
   H. 7
   J. 9
   K. 13

57.

On the number line above, what is the ratio of LM to LN?

   A. 7:11
   B. 5:9
   C. 7:4
   D. 4:5
   E. 2:3

CONTINUE ▶

58. x is a positive integer such that when $x + 2$ is divided by 6, the remainder is 5. What is the remainder when $2x + 2$ is divided by 6?

    F. 5
    G. 4
    H. 3
    J. 2
    K. 1

59. Simplify the expression

$$\frac{m+n}{mn}\left[\left(\frac{n^2}{m}\right)\left(\frac{m^2}{n-m}\right)\right], \text{where}$$

$m \neq n$, $m \neq 0$, and $n \neq 0$.

    A. ^-n
    B. 1
    C. $m + n$
    D. $m^2 + n^2$
    E. $n^2 - m$

60.

Laboratory Bacteria Count

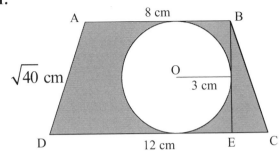

Between which of the following time intervals does the bacteria count show the greatest percent increase?

    F. Hours 1 and 2
    G. Hours 2 and 3
    H. Hours 3 and 5
    J. Hours 4 and 6
    K. Hours 5 and 7

61.

ABCD is an isosceles trapezoid with bases of lengths 8 and 12 cm. Circle O, which is inscribed in ABCD, has a radius of 3 cm. Segment $\overline{BE}$ is tangent to circle O. Find the area of the shaded region.

    A. $3(20 - 3\pi)$ cm^2
    B. $3(40 - 3\pi)$ cm^2
    C. $6(10 - \pi)$ cm^2
    D. $10 - 3\pi$ cm^2
    E. $20 - 9\pi$ cm^2

62. If $3(2x - 5y) + 4 = 7y - 5x + 37$, what is the value of x in terms of y?

    F. $13(y - 2)$
    G. $11(y + 2)$
    H. $7y + 41$
    J. $2y + 3$
    K. $y + 23$

63. Gina is g years old now and Mina is 8 years older. How old was Mina 13 years ago, in terms of g?

    A. $g + 21$
    B. $g + 15$
    C. $g - 13$
    D. $g - 8$
    E. $g - 5$

CONTINUE ▶

64.

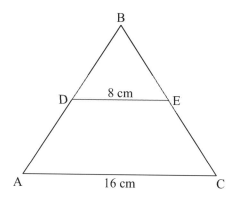

ABC is an isosceles triangle with a base of 16 cm. Points D and E are the midpoints of segments $\overline{AB}$ and $\overline{BC}$, respectively. $\overline{DE}$ has a length of 8 cm. If $\angle BDE \cong \angle BAC$ and the area of trapezoid ADEC is 72 cm², what is the area of triangle ABC?

F. 24 sq cm
G. 39 sq cm
H. 48 sq cm
J. 96 sq cm
K. 192 sq cm

65. If the number 1,365,787 is squared, which digit will be in the tens place?

A. 3
B. 4
C. 6
D. 7
E. 9

66. Alex spent c cents on snacks at a store. If Sam spent $c + 4$ **dollars** on snacks, how much did they spend altogether on snacks, in cents?

F. $4(50.5c + 1)$
G. $101c + 400$
H. $100(c + 4)$
J. $99c + 400$
K. $2c + 4$

67. If a perfectly circular tire spins exactly 1500 times as the car travels 7,065 feet, what is the best approximation of the diameter of the tire?

A. 1.5 inches
B. 4.71 inches
C. 9.42 inches
D. 18 inches
E. 23.2 inches

68. If $\dfrac{7(q - r)}{5}$ is a positive integer, where q is positive and $r = 6$, what is the smallest possible value of q?

F. 3
G. 5
H. 7
J. 9
K. 11

69. Tammy scored a 56, 67, and 91 on three tests. After her fourth test, her average for the four tests was a 73. What was her score on the fourth test?

A. 74
B. 77
C. 78
D. 83
E. 89

70. There are 78 students in the 8th grade class. If the ratio of girls to boys is 8:5, how many fewer boys are there in the class?

F. 13
G. 18
H. 26
J. 33
K. 48

CONTINUE ▶

71. What is the difference between $\sqrt{5^2}+\sqrt{12^2}$ and $\sqrt{5^2+12^2}$?

    A. 0
    B. 1
    C. 2
    D. 3
    E. 4

72. If Grover buys x staplers at \$2.50 each and y hole punchers at \$3.33 each, for a total of \$32.48, how many items did he buy in total?

    F. 12
    G. 11
    H. 10
    J. 9
    K. 7

73. Let $r \mathrel{\Xi} s = \dfrac{r-2s}{4}$, for all values of r and s. What is the value of $r \mathrel{\Xi} (s \mathrel{\Xi} s)$, when $r = 6$ and $s = 8$?

    A. 0
    B. 2.5
    C. 4
    D. 5.25
    E. 6.5

74. Ricky has 20 crayons. 8 are blue, 5 are red, 6 are green, and the rest are yellow. If he reaches for a crayon randomly, what is the probability that he will get either a blue or yellow crayon?

    F. 0.55
    G. 0.5
    H. 0.45
    J. 0.35
    K. 0.25

75. $5z(6w - 7) =$

    A. $30zw - 35z$
    B. $11zw - 12z$
    C. $11zw - 2z$
    D. $23zw$
    E. ^{-}zw

76. Because of breakthroughs in technology, 4 workers are able to build 6 houses in 540 hours. At this rate, how many more men would be needed if 6 houses are to be built in 10 days?

    F. 9
    G. 5
    H. 4
    J. 2
    K. 1

77. Quentin averaged 4.62 seconds on the 40-yard dash across five trials. If his first four times, in seconds, are 4.7, 4.61, 4.65, and 4.59, what is the difference between his final time and his median time?

    A. 0 seconds
    B. 0.02 seconds
    C. 0.03 seconds
    D. 0.05 seconds
    E. 0.06 seconds

78. $\{2, 4, 6, \ldots, 200, 202, 204\}$

What is the sum of all the elements in the set above?

    F. 2,006
    G. 4,012
    H. 6,936
    J. 10,506
    K. 21,012

CONTINUE ▶

79. There are two cubits in one yard, and ¼ of a yard in one span. How many times a span is a cubit?

A. $\dfrac{1}{2}$

B. $\dfrac{1}{4}$

C. $\dfrac{1}{8}$

D. 2

E. 4

80. A fishing boat caught 5446 fish. The fish were distributed as evenly as possible, in whole number quantities, among the 386 people in the village. What is the difference between how many fish each person received and how many fish remained after the distribution?

F. 0
G. 7
H. 14
J. 21
K. 28

81. Juan jogged $5\dfrac{7}{13}$ miles. Yasmin jogged $2\dfrac{8}{9}$ times as many miles as Juan did. How many miles did Yasmin jog?

A. $7\dfrac{15}{22}$

B. $10\dfrac{56}{117}$

C. 16

D. 17

E. $17\dfrac{2}{3}$

82. Jeremy bought 9 watermelons for $48.24. He wants to sell 5 of them and wants to make back at least 80% of his total cost. What is the lowest price, rounded to the nearest cent, at which he can sell each watermelon, assuming he sells each watermelon at the same price?

F. $6.98
G. $7.72
H. $9.12
J. $9.93
K. $10.45

83. The sum of five consecutive odd integers is 155. What is the greatest of these integers?

A. 27
B. 31
C. 35
D. 37
E. 41

84.

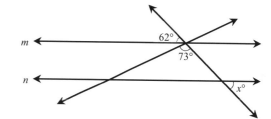

In the figure above, lines m and n are parallel. There are 3 points of intersection in the system of the 4 lines shown, including the two unlabeled lines. What is value of x?

F. 45
G. 62
H. 73
J. 118
K. 135

CONTINUE ▶

85.

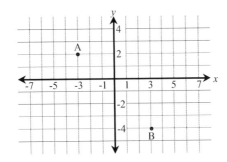

If points A and B were connected by a line segment, what would be the segment's length?

A. 6 units

B. $6\sqrt{2}$ units

C. 7 units

D. $7\sqrt{3}$ units

E. 12 units

86. The probability of picking a red straw from a container of 40 straws is 12.5%. How many non-red straws should be added to the container to decrease the probability of picking a red straw to 4%?

F. 85

G. 75

H. 70

J. 55

K. 24

87. K is an element of the set {3, 4, 5, 6, 7}.

If $\frac{3}{4}K \times \frac{20}{21}$ is an integer, what is K?

A. 3

B. 4

C. 5

D. 6

E. 7

88. Stem-and-Leaf Plot of Daily Temperatures in a 20-Day Span

6	8 8 9 9
7	2 3 3 4 5 8
8	0 1 2 2 6 6
9	2 8 9
10	3

What is the median temperature in the 20-day span?

F. 74

G. 75

H. 78

J. 79

K. 80

89. There are 5,400 birds on island. Of the birds, there are twice as many finches as there are canaries. There are also 1.5 times as many female finches as there are male finches. How many birds are not female finches?

A. 1,440

B. 1,800

C. 2,160

D. 3,240

E. 4,060

90. An isosceles right triangle has a hypotenuse whose length is $7\sqrt{2}$ cm. If one of the other edges of the triangle shares a side with a square, what is the area of the square?

F. $14\sqrt{2}$ cm²

G. 24.5 cm²

H. 35 cm²

J. 49 cm²

K. 98 cm²

CONTINUE ▶

91. If Y is an even integer, which of the following must be true?

    A. $Y(Y - 1)$ is odd.

    B. $\dfrac{Y}{2} + 2$ is even.

    C. $Y + 1$ is prime.

    D. $2Y + 1$ is divisible by 3.

    E. $(Y - 1)^2$ is odd.

92. On a map, ½-inch represents 75 miles. How many square inches on the map represent 100 square miles?

    F. $\dfrac{1}{15^2}$

    G. $\dfrac{1}{75^2}$

    H. $\dfrac{1}{150^2}$

    J. 100

    K. 150^2

93. Andreas received a birthday gift in a box that measured 10 inches long, 0.75 **feet** wide, and 4 inches tall. How much space did the box occupy?

    A. $\dfrac{5}{24}$ cu ft

    B. 2.5 cu ft

    C. 3 cu ft

    D. 30 cu ft

    E. 360 cu ft

94. If g represents the value of 1.0684 rounded to the nearest hundredth, what is the value of $1.0684 + g$?

    F. 2.136
    G. 2.1368
    H. 2.1384
    J. 2.14
    K. 2.156

95. Find the value of $(x^2 + y^2)(^-y^2 + x^2)$, if $x = 2$ and $y = 3$?

    A. $^-65$
    B. $^-5$
    C. 0
    D. 9
    E. 13

96. A dog is tied by a 5-foot rope to the middle of a square barn's wall, which measures 30 feet. What is the perimeter of the area the dog can roam?

    F. 5π ft

    G. 10π ft

    H. $10 + 5\pi$ ft

    J. $10 + 12.5\pi$ ft

    K. 12.5π ft

97. A botanist picked 35 roses at random from a field of 1,000 roses. 18 were red, 10 were pink, and the remainder were white. About how many white roses are in the field?

    A. 700
    B. 625
    C. 500
    D. 350
    E. 200

CONTINUE ▶

98. In an *x,y*-coordinate plane, an equilateral triangle has side lengths of 5 units. It has a vertex at the origin and another one at point (5, 0). Which of the following could be coordinates for the third vertex?

F. $\left(\dfrac{5}{2}, 5\sqrt{2}\right)$

G. $\left(\dfrac{5}{2}, -\dfrac{5\sqrt{3}}{2}\right)$

H. (0, 5)

J. (5, 0)

K. $\left(\dfrac{5}{2}, \dfrac{5}{2}\right)$

99.

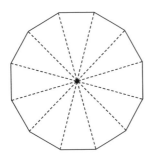

A regular dodecahedron is shown above. What is the sum of the dodecahedron's interior angles, which are only those angles formed by the polygon's edges and vertices? (Hint: a circle has 360°.)

A. 2450°
B. 1800°
C. 900°
D. 150°
E. 75°

100. If a one-gallon can of paint provides enough paint for 10 square yards, how many cans will have to be opened to cover 2000 square feet?

F. 20
G. 21
H. 22
J. 23
K. 200

STOP. THIS IS THE END OF THE TEST. IF TIME PERMITS, YOU MAY REVIEW YOUR ANSWERS TO PARTS 1 AND 2 OF THE TEST.

SHSAT
TJHSST EDITION
TEST 3

PART 1 — VERBAL

Suggested Time — 60 Minutes
45 QUESTIONS

SCRAMBLED PARAGRAPHS

PARAGRAPHS 1-5

DIRECTIONS: The purpose of this section is to organize sentences into the best six-sentence paragraphs possible. For each paragraph, the first sentence is provided, but the remaining five are presented in random or no particular order. Re-order and organize these five sentences, if necessary, to create the **most** logical paragraph. Each paragraph is worth **two** points, whereas every other question type in this test is worth one. Partial credit will not be given.

Blanks have been provided to help you keep track of the position of each sentence in the paragraph. For instance, if you think a sentence follows the first, given sentence, write "2" in the blank next to it; write "3" next to the sentence that you believe follows "2"; and so on. When you believe you have arranged the sentences correctly, transfer your response to your answer sheet.

Paragraph 1

Intel has always been a critical component of national strategy—the more information you have, the better positioned you potentially are to protect and promote your interests.

_____ **Q.** Prior to the CIA, there was no semblance of a central intelligence agency until President Franklin D. Roosevelt appointed William Donovan as Coordinator of Information.

_____ **R.** Up until then, each branch of the military and government conducted its own intelligence-related operations; President Roosevelt hoped to change this by establishing the Office of Strategic Services (OSS) in 1942, the following year.

_____ **S.** It was not until after the OSS was dissolved in 1945, and its duties and functions were consequently further decentralized, that the importance of a truly centralized intelligence agency became apparent.

_____ **T.** Even with the establishment of the OSS, however, many agencies still maintained their own separate intelligence activities.

_____ **U.** Today, the Central Intelligence Agency, or CIA, which was established by President Truman when he signed the National Security Act of 1947, is one of our nation's mainstays in gathering and analyzing intel.

CONTINUE ▶

Paragraph 2

Stretching more than 5,000 miles across in length, the Great Wall of China remains one of the most ambitious manmade construction undertakings of all time.

_____   **Q.**   After the fall of the Qin dynasty in 206 B.C., much of the Great Wall fell into a state of disrepair, with only segments of it being occasionally repaired for the benefit of the tribes or faction controlling the said segments at the time.

_____   **R.**   In the ensuing years, the Wall lost much of its military significance, most notably after Genghis Khan's Yuan (Mongol) Dynasty took control of China from 1206 to 1368 A.D.

_____   **S.**   Construction of the Great Wall is said to have commenced sometime around 220 B.C. at the commission of Emperor Qin Shi Huang, who served as the first emperor of a unified China that was comprised of the previously individual kingdoms from earlier periods.

_____   **T.**   Over 100 years passed before construction of the Great Wall of China, as we know it, began again in earnest, around 1474, during the rule of the Ming Dynasty.

_____   **U.**   Emperor Qin ordered that many of the pre-existing fortifications and walls built between the kingdoms or states be joined into a single system, but work on the Wall would be relatively short-lived.

Paragraph 3

Lacrosse, with its 70,000 or so high school participants, may seem a fledgling sport when compared to the likes of some others, such as football, which draws 1.1 million high school athletes annually.

_____   **Q.**   It may not be as popular as some sports are now, but it is anything but fledgling—quite the opposite is true; lacrosse is North America's oldest indigenous sport.

_____   **R.**   Later, in the mid-1800's, Europeans also became increasingly involved in lacrosse, and in 1867, William George Beers standardized the game of lacrosse, limiting the number of players and establishing other rules, effectively ushering in modern lacrosse.

_____   **S.**   For these tribes and others, lacrosse was more than a game—it was also a culturally symbolic affair, often used as a means of conflict resolution, healing, and thanksgiving.

_____   **T.**   While the details of lacrosse's origination remain scant—the first European documentation was made by French Jesuit missionaries in the 1630s—it is thought that lacrosse was invented by the Huron and Iroquois tribes in the early 15th century.

_____   **U.**   Lacrosse games were massive affairs, commonly involving anywhere from hundreds to thousands of players and lasting up to a few days, which may have been necessary, given that the playing fields, which used natural boundaries, could stretch for miles.

CONTINUE ▶

Paragraph 4

Ladybugs or ladybird beetles, as the insects of the family *Coccinellidae* are most familiarly known, can be a valuable resource and aide for farmers and other agriculturists.

_____ **Q.** Instantly recognizable for their polka-dotted, bright red shells—*coccineus* means "scarlet" in Latin—many species of this beetle are especially useful to farmers who want to avoid the use of harmful pesticides because they prey on crop-damaging pests.

_____ **R.** And, fortunately, a ladybug's diet doesn't change from its larval stage to its adult stage, which allows for even further aphid population control.

_____ **S.** Because ladybugs feed voraciously on plant-eating pests, such as aphids, that could severely damage or ruin crops, the species *Harmonia axyridis* was imported from Asia in 1988 to control aphid populations.

_____ **T.** Unfortunately, while these imported ladybugs have assisted with aphid population control, without a natural predator, they have overrun North America and have also pervaded into Europe, and signs of disrupted ecosystems are already emerging.

_____ **U.** In fact, "voracious" might be an understatement for a ladybug's appetite; a single ladybug reportedly eats over 5,000 aphids during its larval stage alone.

Paragraph 5

Adapted into 20 international versions and aired in over 120 countries worldwide, *Sesame Street* is one of the biggest, if not the biggest, children's television programming phenomena in history.

_____ **Q.** And a fun, but educational, program was just what was needed to turn around the American television landscape at the time, which FCC chairman Newton Minow described as a "wasteland" in 1961.

_____ **R.** This international cultural phenomenon was conceived of in 1966 by Joan Ganz Cooney, a former documentary producer, to leverage the addictive power of television and use it to promote a good cause for a change.

_____ **S.** She wanted to use the addictiveness of television to provide young audiences with a fun way to learn and help them prepare for kindergarten.

_____ **T.** Almost immediately upon airing, the show was a rousing success, and it has continued to be a success—in its 43 years of being on air, *Sesame Street* has won numerous awards, but more importantly, it has exceeded the educational impact that it set out to have.

_____ **U.** So after two years of research and development, and a grant of $8 million from various sources, the first telecast of *Sesame Street* was aired on November 10, 1969.

CONTINUE ▶

LOGICAL REASONING
QUESTIONS 11-25

DIRECTIONS: For each question, read the information provided and select the **best** answer choice, based **only on the information given.** In other words, even if you know more about a particular set of facts than is provided, do not use outside facts to aid your decision-making process.

When dealing with logical reasoning questions, be on alert for certain placement or position and order words and phrases, such as **to the right of**, **above**, **before**, and **next to**. "The puppy is **between** the kitten and duckling," for instance, is not necessarily the same as "The puppy is **between and next to** the kitten and duckling"; one or more other objects may separate the puppy from the kitten or from the duckling.

---

11. If I am full, I will not eat. If I eat, I will drink soda.

    Based only on the information above, which of the following **must** be true?

    A. If I drink soda, I am not full.
    B. If I drink soda, I am eating.
    C. If I do not eat, I am full.
    D. If I do not drink soda, I am full.
    E. If I eat, I am not full and I will drink soda.

12. Everyone in Puntsville is good at kicking a football. Some people in Puntsville can kick a field goal from 60 yards away. Everyone who can kick a field goal from 60 yards away can run a 5-minute mile.

    Based only on the information above, which of the following **must** be true?

    F. Everyone who can run a 5-minute mile is good at kicking a football.
    G. Everyone who can run a 5-minute mile can kick a field goal from 60 yards.
    H. Everyone in Puntsville can run a 5-minute mile.
    J. Everyone who can kick a field goal from 60 yards away is also good at kicking a football.
    K. Some people in Puntsville can run a 5-minute mile.

13. 51 cops and robbers sit in a circle. Cops always tell the truth, and robbers always lie. With the exception of one, who says, "A cop is to my right," everyone else says, "A robber is to my right." How many cops there are?

    A. 23
    B. 24
    C. 25
    D. 26
    E. Cannot be determined from the information given.

14. Cheetahs can accelerate from 0 to 60 miles per hour in 3 seconds. The Ferrari Enzo, one of the fastest accelerating cars in the world, does 0 to 60 miles per hour in 3.4 seconds.

    Based only on the information above, which of the following **must** be true?

    F. Cheetahs can never outrace a Ferrari.
    G. All cars are slower than cheetahs.
    H. Cheetahs are the fastest land animals.
    J. Cheetahs accelerate from 0 to 30 miles per hour faster than the Ferrari Enzo.
    K. Cheetahs can accelerate from 0 to 60 miles per hour at least as fast as one of the world's fastest accelerating cars.

CONTINUE ▶

15. Mika is arranging her clothes in her closet. Each article of clothing has a different color.

   1) Mika places the jacket first.
   2) Mika places the turquoise article of clothing before the pink one.
   3) The violet article of clothing is second, and two articles of clothing separate the violet one from the magenta one.
   4) Mika places the gown immediately before the sundress, which is turquoise.

If the blouse comes before the coat, what color is the coat?

   A. Turquoise
   B. Pink
   C. Lavender
   D. Magenta
   E. Violet

16. Shawna likes to read at least one novel per week. There are four genres of literature she likes to read: mystery, romance, historical fiction, and biographies.

   1) If she reads a mystery novel, she will not read a biography.
   2) If she reads a romance novel, she will not read a historical fiction novel.
   3) If she reads a biography, she will read neither a romance novel nor a historical fiction novel.

If Shawna reads a mystery novel, what other genre, if any, can she read in the same week?

   I.   Romance
   II. Historical Fiction
   III. Biography

   F. I and II
   G. II and III
   H. I or II, but not both
   J. II or III, but not both
   K. I, II, and II

17. A photographer is taking a picture of 6 students in a human pyramid, with 3 students at the base, 2 students in the middle row, and 1 at the top.

   1) Carrie is at the top of the pyramid.
   2) Pete is somewhere to Bart's left, from Bart's perspective, on the same row.
   3) The photographer sees Jake somewhere to the left of Doug, on the same row.

Based only on the information above, how many possible spots can Kirk occupy in the pyramid?

   A. 2
   B. 3
   C. 4
   D. 5
   E. 6

18. The smartest kid in my school can read 25 novels in a week. I can read 25 novels in a week.

Based only on the information above, which of the following **must** be true?

   F. If I am not the smartest kid, then how many novels a kid can read in a week is not the measure of smartness being used.
   G. I am the smartest kid in my school.
   H. No one else in my school can read 25 novels in a week.
   J. If I am the smartest kid in my school, no other kid in my school can read 25 or more novels in a week.
   K. I am one of the smartest kids in my school.

CONTINUE ▶

19. On his way to work, Tom passes six different animals.

1) He passes the cat first.
2) He passes the dog before he passes the bird, which he passes before the squirrel.
3) He passes the lizard immediately before he passes the fox.

Based only on the information above, how many different possible orders of animals are there?

A. 5
B. 4
C. 3
D. 2
E. 1

20. Yancy works five days a week. He either walks, bikes, or drives to work, but he never goes to work using the same mode of transportation more than twice per week. And if he walks to work, he takes the bus home.

In a span of four weeks, what is the difference between the least and greatest number of times Yancy can take the bus home?

F. 1
G. 2
H. 3
J. 4
K. 6

21. Every mountain in Heightsland is taller than any mountain in Peaksland. Mount Juneau is in Peaksland and is not as tall as Mount Yaro.

Based only on the information above, which of the following **must** be true?

A. Mount Yaro is not in Heightsland.
B. Mount Yaro is not in Peaksland.
C. If Mount Juneau is the tallest mountain in Peaksland, then Mount Yaro is in Heightsland.
D. Mount Yaro is taller than any mountain in Peaksland.
E. If Mount Juneau is the tallest mountain in Peaksland, then Mount Yaro is not in Peaksland.

22. Five students race to the school bus.

1) Soleil gets to the bus first.
2) Macy reaches the bus immediately before Rita does.
3) Three students separate Soleil and Priscilla, who reaches the bus immediately after Nancy does.

What is the correct order of the students, from first to last, as they reach the bus?

F. Soleil, Nancy, Macy, Rita, Priscilla
G. Soleil, Nancy, Macy, Priscilla, Rita
H. Soleil, Macy, Nancy, Rita, Priscilla
J. Soleil, Macy, Rita, Nancy, Priscilla
K. Soleil, Nancy, Priscilla, Macy, Rita

CONTINUE ▶

23. At a school fun fair, five students—Ashton, Brandi, Kara, Leno, and Otto—were assigned to five different booths, which were numbered from 1 to 5.

1) Leno was assigned to booth 5.
2) Kara had the comics booth, which had a smaller number than the stickers booth.
3) Brandi's ice cream booth had a bigger number than the music booth, which had a bigger number than that of the stickers booth.

Based only on the information above, which of the following **could** be true?

A. The comics booth's number was 2.
B. The ice cream booth's number was 3.
C. Ashton's booth's number was 2.
D. Otto's booth's number was 1.
E. The music booth's number was 1.

Questions 24 and 25 refer to the following information.

In the code below, (1) each letter always represents the same word, (2) each word is represented by only one letter, and (3) in any given sentence, the letters may or may not be presented in the same order as the words.

P	X	R	O	L	means
"Mick	sings	a	happy	song."	
M	O	K	W	P	means
"Chu	hums	a	happy	tune."	
R	X	L	Y	O	means
"Katie	sings	Mick	a	song."	
Z	K	O	Q	N	means
"Han	whistles	a	jolly	tune."	

24. Which letter represents the word "Katie"?

F. Y
G. P
H. L
J. K
K. Cannot be determined from the information given.

25. How many letters could be assigned to more than one word?

A. 8
B. 7
C. 6
D. 5
E. 3

CONTINUE ▶

READING

QUESTIONS 26-50

DIRECTIONS: Each passage below has five questions associated with it. After reading a passage, answer the questions, based **only on the information provided** by the passage; even if you have a deeper knowledge of the contents of the passage, do not base your answers on any outside knowledge.

On May 22, 1960, an earthquake that registered 9.5 on the Richter scale rocked the coast of South Central Chile, killing over 1,600, injuring another 3,000, and leaving 2 million homeless.
5   That wasn't all. The Chilean earthquake, which was the world's largest recorded earthquake, also triggered a Pacific-wide tsunami that killed over 200 in Hawaii, Japan, and the Philippines combined. The tsunami alone caused over half a
10 billion dollars' worth of damage worldwide.

When an earthquake occurs, it generates seismic waves, which are the vibrations that emanate from the earthquake's hypocenter or origination point. The seismic waves are recorded by seis-
15 mographs as a series of zigzags. But because the amplitudes of seismic waves can differ by orders of magnitude, Charles F. Richter devised the Richter magnitude scale, which is based on a logarithmic scale, in 1935 as a way to compare
20 the sizes of earthquakes.

The Richter scale simplifies tracking and measuring seismic activity, but it can also lead to a misunderstanding of how significant each point on the scale is. In terms of seismic wave ampli-
25 tude, each point of increase represents a tenfold increase in seismic wave amplitude—an increase in three points on the Richter scale represents a thousand-fold increase in seismic wave amplitude. Furthermore, in terms of an earthquake's
30 energy, each point of increase represents a 31.6-fold increase in the amount of energy released. This makes, for example, a difference of two points on the Richter scale tantamount to a difference of about 1,000 times the energy release.

35 Based on this information, it would be reasonable to surmise that the aforementioned earthquake to hit Chile was the most devastating, but this was not the case. On January 12, 2010, an earthquake struck Haiti that killed over 316,000
40 and injured another 300,000. What's somewhat surprising is how this much tamer earthquake—it registered 7.0 on the Richter scale—was much more ruthless in its blatant disregard for life.

The only logical conclusion that can be made of
45 these seemingly contradictory facts is that the strength of an earthquake is not the only factor in determining its destructive potential. Surrounding population density, geographic features, and architectural landscape, among other
50 things, also help to determine an earthquake's destructive potential.

26. What is the author's purpose for writing this passage?

F. to argue that the Richter scale is not a good indicator of how catastrophic earthquakes can be
G. to praise Charles Richter for coming up with an efficient way of measuring the strength of earthquakes
H. to compare and contrast two earthquakes and the impact that they had
J. to point out that earthquakes are unrivaled as far as devastating natural phenomena go
K. to demystify earthquakes and what contributes to their destructive potential

CONTINUE ▶

27. Based on the passage, about how many times the energy of an earthquake measuring 5.0 on the Richter scale would an earthquake measuring 9.0 release?

A. 40
B. 10,000
C. 31,600
D. 1,000,000
E. 40,000,000

28. Which of the following is not mentioned as contributing to an earthquake's destructive potential?

F. population density
G. geographic features
H. architectural landscape
J. hypocenter location
K. earthquake strength

29. According to the passage, about how many deaths did the Chilean earthquake of May 22, 1960 cause, whether directly or indirectly?

A. 1,600
B. 3,000
C. 1,800
D. 4,600
E. over 2 million

30. Which of the following is most strongly supported by the passage?

F. Even microquakes—earthquakes that register 2.0 or lower on the Richter scale—can be devastating under the right circumstances.
G. The Richter scale was developed because scientists were having a difficult time recording seismic wave activity.
H. If Haiti had been hit by the same earthquake that had hit Chile in 1960, millions of lives would have been lost.
J. All earthquakes over 9.0 on the Richter scale generate tsunamis.
K. The Chilean earthquake of 1960 caused over 2 billion dollars' worth of damage.

CONTINUE ▶

Christopher Columbus, Vasco da Gama, and Amerigo Vespucci have all been memorialized in history for "discovering" foreign lands. Comparatively, Norwegian explorer Roald Amund-
5   sen is not as well known, but that does not mean he was any less adventurous or courageous.

Roald Engebreth Gravning Amundsen was born in Borge, Norway, in 1862, into a family of merchant sea captains and wealthy ship owners and
10 knew from a young age that he would embark on polar explorations, thus prompting him to condition himself for arctic climates by sleeping with his window open at nights. And, later on, when he laid eyes for the first time on Antarctica's
15 glacial walls in 1897, he knew he wanted to be the first to set foot on the frozen southern continent.

Originally, he had wanted to be the first to reach the North Pole and began making preparations
20 accordingly in 1909. But when he learned that American Robert Peary had accomplished this feat—it was later discovered, rather ironically, that Peary may have falsified his report when scholars realized that Peary's described route
25 and timeframe for getting to the North Pole were nigh impossible—Amundsen instead rechanneled his efforts on sailing to Antarctica.

After returning to Norway from successfully navigating through Canada's Northwest Passage,
30 Amundsen learned that a contemporary of his named Ernest Shackleton had set out for Antarctica. Shackleton was forced to turn back just 97 miles short of the South Pole, after having made landfall on Antarctica, and so Amundsen took
35 the opportunity to study as much of Shackleton's attempt as he could. After much preparation, Amundsen and his crew set out for Antarctica in the June of 1910.

They reached the Bay of Whales in early Janu-
40 ary 1911 and from there set out for the South Pole on October 18 of the same year. Almost two months later, on December 14, 1911, Amundsen raised the Norwegian flag at the South Pole, and he and his crew returned safely
45 to their base camp. He went on to become the

first to fly over the North Pole in 1926, in a dirigible. And if Peary had indeed falsified his reports of his Arctic expedition, Amundsen would also be the first to reach the North Pole.

31.   What is the main idea of the passage?

    A.   Roald Amundsen should be as well-known as at least other major explorers.
    B.   Robert Peary falsified his travel data and cannot be regarded as the first to reach the North Pole.
    C.   Everyone should have a goal he or she is passionate about accomplishing or obtaining.
    D.   Roald Amundsen, not Robert Peary, was the first to reach the North Pole.
    E.   Roald Amundsen accomplished much as a polar explorer.

32.   How did Roald Amundsen train, at an early age, to become a polar explorer?

    F.   He frequently accompanied his parents on overseas expeditions.
    G.   He slept with his window open during the winters.
    H.   He observed his father, who was ship owner and merchant sea captain, very carefully, as his father commanded various crews.
    J.   He studied the notes and records of other explorers to help him figure out what he needed to do as an explorer.
    K.   He honed his skills as a polar explorer by gradually increasing the difficulty of his expeditions, which is why he sailed the Northwest Passage before attempting Antarctica.

CONTINUE ▶

33. How was it likely determined that Robert Peary may have falsified his claims of being the first to reach the North Pole?

   A. There was absolutely no way that Peary could have reached the North Pole in the way and timeframe he claimed, even if he had flown there by airplane.
   B. Peary admitted at a later date that he had falsified his records and also admitted that Amundsen's 1926 flight marked the first time anyone had reached the North Pole.
   C. Peary's described route and timeframe were nearly impossible to replicate by scholars and other sailors.
   D. When later scholars got to the North Pole, they saw Amundsen's dirigible, but no American flag planted there.
   E. In 1909, ships that could sail through polar waters had not yet been invented.

34. Which of the following is the least supported by the passage?

   F. Roald Amundsen was the first to reach Antarctica.
   G. Had Amundsen known that Peary's records had been falsified, he may not have sailed to Antarctica.
   H. Roald Amundsen was 34 or 35 years of age when he first saw the continent of Antarctica.
   J. Mishaps or tragedies forced Ernest Shackleton to abandon trying to reach the South Pole.
   K. It took Amundsen and his crew almost 60 days to reach the South Pole, after having reached the Bay of Whales.

35. Which of the following would the author most likely agree with about Roald Amundsen?

   A. He wanted to be the first to accomplish an exploration feat of some sort.
   B. He would have become clinically depressed if he was denied the chance at being first to the South Pole.
   C. He spent over a year preparing for his expedition to Antarctica.
   D. He was the one who named the Bay of Whales and did so because he witnessed hundreds of whales taking shelter there.
   E. He flew over the North Pole in a dirigible because the airplane had not yet been invented.

CONTINUE ▶

From 1982 to 2012, there have been over 60 mass murders that were carried out using at least one firearm, and in almost 50 of them, the killer, or killers, had obtained his weapon(s) legally—
5 2012 alone saw 13 shootings that resulted in the deaths of multiple people. The United States also has the highest rate of guns per capita, with 90 guns per every 100 citizens, on average, according to the Small Arms Survey 2007, a study
10 released by the Graduate Institute of International Studies. Why is a culture of firearms so firmly entrenched in this country? The background of the Second Amendment, which grants citizens the right to bear arms and which was
15 ratified as a part of the Bill of Rights on December 15, 1791, may shed some insight.

After James II ascended the throne of England in 1685 as a Catholic—England's officially established church was the Church of England—he
20 began promoting Catholicism in various ways, such as appointing Catholics to military and government positions and mandating religious equality between Protestants and Catholics. Moreover, he made moves to establish himself
25 as an absolute monarch, which caused additional tension with Parliament. This tension culminated in James's deposition in late 1688 by his daughter Mary and her husband William of Orange, both of whom were Protestants.

30 As a condition to succeeding the crown of England, William and Mary were required by Parliament to accept the English Bill of Rights of 1689, which was designed to correct the abuses of power by King James II and to better define
35 and guarantee the rights of the English people. Among the rights protected is the right of "the subjects [to] have arms for their defense suitable to their conditions and as allowed by law."

Naturally, the American colonists shared many
40 of the same views on life and liberty as the English did, so when King George III of England began imposing oppressive requirements on the American colonists, it is no surprise that they snapped and revolted, which ultimately led to
45 our own Bill of Rights, which in turn has either directly or indirectly played some extent of a role for our gun culture to thrive and persist.

36. What was the author's main purpose for writing this passage?

F. to urge that the Second Amendment be repealed, in light of the recent shootings
G. to provide an overview of the English Bill of Rights
H. to prove that the rift between the Catholic Church and the Church of England fueled modern-day gun use
J. to suggest a causal link between the history of the Second Amendment and the prevalence of guns in society
K. to explain how King James II was overthrown by his daughter and her husband

37. In what year was James II deposed of as king?

A. 1685
B. 1688
C. 1689
D. 1791
E. 1982

38. According to the passage, what was one of the purposes of the English Bill of Rights?

F. to deny future kings the right to bear arms
G. to make it impossible for the government to engage in taxation without representation
H. to prevent abuses of power by future kings
J. to establish laws that would prevent English subjects from rebelling against the government
K. to partially guarantee and protect the rights of the English people

CONTINUE ▶

39. Which of the following is implied by the passage?

   A. If William and Mary had not accepted the English Bill of Rights, Parliament would have taken over the entirety of the English governance process, seeing how there would be no monarch immediately available to replace James II.

   B. It is only because of the English Bill of Rights that American colonists had any idea about what rights they felt should be guaranteed and protected.

   C. At the time of James II's reign, English monarchs did not have absolute power over the nation.

   D. If King George III had not oppressed the American colonists, the United States would still be under the British crown.

   E. More than three-fourths of England's populace was Protestant.

40. Which of the following statements would the author most likely agree with?

   F. If guns are made unavailable to the public, mass killings will forever cease to occur.

   G. Guns are pure evil and serve no useful purpose to society.

   H. 90% of America's population owns guns.

   J. If James II had not promoted Catholicism by promoting Catholics to various official positions, he would not have been ousted from the throne.

   K. William and Mary were in some way connected to Parliament at the time James II was overthrown.

CONTINUE ▶

The name Stephen King is almost synonymous with the horror genre. With over 60 books published and over 350 million copies of his books sold worldwide, as of 2006—*Carrie*, his first
5 novel, by itself sold over 4 million copies soon after its publication in the spring of 1974—and numerous awards to his name, Stephen King is, in his own right, an international celebrity.

Before he rose to prominence, King was an ordi-
10 nary person, who lived with his wife in a trailer. Upon graduating from Lisbon Falls High School in 1966, King matriculated at the University of Maine at Orono. He graduated as an English major in 1970 and received his teaching certificate,
15 but he was not able to secure a job as a teacher until later. Instead, he worked odd jobs until he was hired to teach at Hampden Academy in the fall of 1971. Throughout college and thereafter, King wrote short stories while working on ideas
20 for novels; he managed to sell some of his short stories, his first one being "The Glass Door," which sold in 1967 to *Startling Mystery Stories*.

Many authors often spend years before they produce a completed manuscript. Harper Lee, for
25 example, spent over two years writing *To Kill a Mockingbird*, which was published in 1960 and became an instant hit, winning the Pulitzer Prize in 1961 and becoming a staple in English curricula all around the country—to date, it has sold
30 over 30 million copies in 18 languages. Harper Lee published nothing after *To Kill a Mockingbird*, though she had begun working on other pieces. Comparing Harper Lee and other authors to Stephen King, and vice versa, can be a flawed
35 process—genre, writing style, personal circumstances, and philosophical approaches to writing all factor into how quickly authors write and their respective levels of commercial success— but Stephen King is undeniably a prolific writer.

40 What's his secret to churning out books so frequently? When interviewed in 1979 by the *New York Times*, he replied, "I'm not a fast writer, but I stick to it. I write 1,500 words a day, and the stuff just piles up." In other words, it re-
45 quires a consistent level of dedication and effort.

41. What is the main purpose of the passage?

    A. to let the readers know that it is possible for anyone to succeed if he puts his mind to it
    B. to tell who Stephen King is and how he is able to write so much
    C. to compare Stephen King with Harper Lee, the Pulitzer Prize winner of *To Kill a Mockingbird*
    D. to emphasize why it is difficult to compare authors
    E. to brag about Stephen King's successes

42. Which of the following is not a stated factor of how quickly an author writes and his or her level of commercial success?

    F. writing style
    G. philosophical approaches to writing
    H. genre
    J. personal circumstances
    K. level of family support

43. According to the passage, how is Stephen King such a prolific writer?

    A. He commits to writing a set number of words per day.
    B. He is able to write prolifically because he was an English major in college.
    C. He began writing early on in his life, so he has more ideas about what to write.
    D. He is a fast writer and sticks to writing 1,500 words per day.
    E. He has a natural talent for writing, which was made apparent by the sale of his first short story while he was still in college.

CONTINUE ▶

44. Which of the following can be inferred from the passage?

    F. Harper Lee was a more prolific writer than Stephen King is.

    G. *To Kill a Mockingbird* was both a commercial and literary success.

    H. *To Kill a Mockingbird* is better than any of Stephen King's works.

    J. An author can be deemed successful only if he or she is able to get an interview with a major newspaper, such as the *New York Times*.

    K. Declaring an author to be successful is a flawed process because everyone has different preferences and circumstances.

45. What is the first work Stephen King sold professionally? (The fonts below have deliberately been normalized.)

    A. Startling Mystery Stories

    B. To Kill a Mockingbird

    C. Carrie

    D. The Glass Door

    E. a short story for the New York Times

CONTINUE ▶

The word "investment" invokes thoughts of stocks, but the truth is that there are many investment vehicles to allow an investor to choose the options that best suits his interests or needs.
5   They come in all shapes, sizes, and forms—real estate acquisitions, savings accounts, certificates of deposit, and business startup involvement are some—and stocks are a part of a category of investment vehicles called securities, which are a
10   type of investment that involves obtaining an ownership interest in or debt obligation from the company being invested in. Despite its label, securities are not without risks, but investing in them does not have to be a gamble. Several fac-
15   tors determine how much risk there is or will be, but the greatest cause of risk is the investor himself and what he wants.

It is therefore important to understand risk management. In the world of securities, there are
20   three common types of securities: bonds, stocks, and mutual funds. Bonds are generally the least risky because they are, in essence, loans. When an investor purchases a bond, he expects to be paid back the full amount with interest. Stocks,
25   which are ownership interests in the companies themselves, by contrast, do not offer any guarantees. Mutual funds pool money from different investors to invest in a portfolio of other securities; they also typically do not offer any guaran-
30   tees on performance. The risk of a mutual fund depends on the riskiness of the securities in its portfolio.

Some other key words to know are *diversification* and *volatility*. Diversification is the act of
35   investing in various securities, akin to what mutual funds do, to minimize losses when the stock price of one company drops. Volatility is a measure of how quickly the price of a stock fluctuates. Thus, the more volatile a stock is, the
40   greater the chance of making a faster, bigger profit—but it can also work the opposite way. It is necessary to remember, regardless of what the investor wants, whether it is to take greater risks to gain faster, greater returns or to play it more
45   safely and cautiously for slower, yet more stable, returns, that careful study and analysis are necessary to minimize the risks inherent in investing.

46.   What is the author's main purpose for this passage?

   F.   to teach about some of the basic concepts of investment, including its risks
   G.   to distinguish between the various types of securities
   H.   to define some key investment terms
   J.   to persuade readers to invest in securities at some point in the future, if they haven't already
   K.   to debunk various myths surrounding risk management

47.   Which of the following is not listed as an investment vehicle?

   A.   stocks
   B.   bonds
   C.   mutual funds
   D.   real estate acquisitions
   E.   business liquidations

48.   According to the passage, what is the greatest source of investment risk?

   F.   the volatility of the stocks and mutual funds being invested in
   G.   oversaturation of the stock market by competing companies
   H.   the lack of diversity
   J.   the investor himself
   K.   overconfidence and impatience

CONTINUE ▶

49. According to the passage, how do bonds differ from stocks?

    A. Bonds represent debt obligations, whereas stocks represent ownership interests.

    B. Bonds offer a full guarantee of investment recovery, whereas stocks only offer a partial guarantee.

    C. Bonds are primarily low risk investment vehicles, whereas stocks are primarily high risk investment vehicles.

    D. Bonds are subject to diversification and volatility, whereas stocks are not.

    E. Bonds are always terrible investments, whereas stocks are always good investments.

50. Which of the following can be inferred from the passage about why investors diversify their portfolios?

    F. Diversification is a way for investors to invest without having to do careful research and analysis, thus helping investors save much time, energy, and even more money.

    G. Diversification completely eliminates the need to worry about stock price volatility.

    H. Diversification reduces risk by spreading the risk of loss across multiple investment vehicles, in the event some of investments lose value.

    J. Diversification prevents investors from getting too greedy and possibly losing a lot more in the future.

    K. Diversification is a way to give many smaller companies a chance to do well with their stocks.

CONTINUE ▶

PART 2 — MATH

Suggested Time — 60 Minutes
50 QUESTIONS

GENERAL INSTRUCTIONS

Solve each problem and select the correct answer from the choices given. If you need space to do your work, you may use the test pages or on paper provided to you. ***DO NOT DO YOUR WORK ON YOUR ANSWER SHEET.***

IMPORTANT NOTES:
  (1) Diagrams may not be drawn to scale. Do not assume information about a diagram, unless it is specifically stated by the problem or on this page or it can be reasoned from the given information.
  (2) Assume that the diagrams exist in a single plane unless otherwise specified by the problem.
  (3) Reduce each fraction answer to the lowest terms unless otherwise specified.

SYMBOLS, FORMULAS, AND REPRESENTATIONS

The following reference chart may be useful as you solve the problems. You may refer to this page during the test.

SYMBOLS   MEANING

$\neq$	is not equal to
$<$	is less than
$>$	is greater than
$\leq$	is less than or equal to
$\geq$	is greater than or equal to
$//$	is parallel to
$\perp$	is perpendicular to

REPRESENTATIONS

Angles are represented by

Right angles are represented by

FORMULAS:

Circle's circumference: $2\pi r$

Total triangle interior angle measure: $180°$

Perimeter of a rectangle: $2l + 2w$

Total quadrilateral interior angle measure: $360°$

AREAS:

Triangles: $\frac{1}{2}bh$

Parallelograms: bh

Trapezoids: $\frac{1}{2}(b_1 + b_2)h$

Circles: πr^2

CONTINUE ▶

MATHEMATICS PROBLEMS

QUESTIONS 51-100

DIRECTIONS: Answer or solve each question or problem. Once you have arrived at the correct answer or come up with a satisfactory answer choice, mark your answer sheet accordingly.

---

51. If $x = -y^3$, which of the following **must** be true?

    A. $x \leq 0$
    B. $x \geq 0$
    C. $y + x \geq x^2 - y$
    D. $x - y^3 \leq 0$
    E. $x + y^3 = 0$

52. 7 boys' mean height is 63 inches. If Byron is 72 inches, how tall are the others combined?

    F. 347
    G. 369
    H. 375
    J. 378
    K. 441

53. Marcia is 11 years old now. 9 years ago, Winona was three times as old as Marcia was then. How old is Winona now?

    A. 15
    B. 16
    C. 17
    D. 18
    E. 21

54. If Benny has 5 different pens, in how many different ways can he arrange them?

    F. 5
    G. 15
    H. 35
    J. 60
    K. 120

55. The sum of all the factors of 66 is equal to which number squared?

    A. 8
    B. 10
    C. 12
    D. 14
    E. 18

56. $4z(7q - 6w) =$

    F. ^-4zqw
    G. $4zq - 4zw$
    H. $11zq - 10zw$
    J. $28zq - 24zw$
    K. $52zq + 13w$

57. A bank applies a two-tiered interest rate to its customers' savings accounts. For accounts with balances of \$0.01 to \$99,999.99, the bank applies a 3% interest rate. For accounts with balances of \$100,000.00 or greater, the bank applies a 2.5% interest rate to the entirety of the balance. How much more would a customer earn in interest by having \$90,000 than \$100,000 in her account?

    A. \$200
    B. \$500
    C. \$700
    D. \$2,000
    E. \$2,700

CONTINUE ▶

97

2

58. What is the difference between the greatest and least prime factors of 2,310?

    F. 5
    G. 7
    H. 8
    J. 9
    K. 10

59.
$$\frac{3 - 2 \times \dfrac{1}{4}}{0.5} =$$

    A. $\dfrac{1}{8}$

    B. $\dfrac{1}{2}$

    C. $\dfrac{3}{4}$

    D. $\dfrac{5}{4}$

    E. 5

60. An expert logger can cut a log into two pieces in 4 minutes. If he cuts a log into six pieces, how many minutes will it take him?

    F. 24
    G. 20
    H. 16
    J. 12
    K. 8

61. How many hours are in 225 seconds?

    A. 0.0375
    B. 0.0625
    C. 0.375
    D. 0.5
    E. 3.75

62. If there were 4 girls to every 3 boys at a summer camp, what percent, rounded to the nearest hundredth, of the campers were girls?

    F. 49.32
    G. 57.14
    H. 75
    J. 88.56
    K. 133.33

63. Kirk and Sofia plan to run on a circular track. They will start together on the track but will run in opposite directions until they meet. The track is 1300 feet around, and Kirk runs 1.5 times as fast as Sofia does. How much will Kirk run before they meet?

    A. 780 feet
    B. 520 feet
    C. 260 feet
    D. 130 feet
    E. 65 feet

64. In a set of 8 consecutive odd integers, the smallest integer is k. In terms of k, what is the median of the set?

    F. $k + 6$
    G. $k + 6.5$
    H. $k + 7$
    J. $k + 7.5$
    K. $k + 8$

65. If $3x - 5y + 7 = 6x + 10y + 4$, what is the value of $2x + 1$ in terms of y?

    A. $^-5y + 1$
    B. $^-7.5y + 2.5$
    C. $10y - 3$
    D. $^-6y - 5$
    E. $^-10y + 3$

CONTINUE ▶

66.
$$f(x) = 4x - 1$$
$$g(x) = 5x + 2$$

Which of the following **must** be true for any positive value of x?

F. $f(x) + g(x)$ is even.
G. $g(x) - f(x)$ is odd.
H. $g(x) - f(x)$ is positive.
J. $f(x) - g(x)$ is positive.
K. $f(x) \times g(x)$ is even.

67. Between which two positive integers does $\sqrt{5^2} + \sqrt{6^2} + \sqrt{5^2 + 6^2}$ fall?

A. 23 and 24
B. 21 and 22
C. 19 and 20
D. 18 and 19
E. 16 and 17

68.

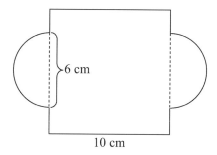

The figure above was constructed by attaching two congruent semicircles of diameter 6 centimeters to a square with a side length of 10 centimeters. If an ant starts at any point and makes its way around the figure back to its starting point, without ever retracing its steps, how much does it walk?

F. $24 + 12\pi$ cm
G. $28 + 6\pi$ cm
H. $40 + 9\pi$ cm
J. $100 + 9\pi$ cm
K. $100 + 36\pi$ cm

69.
$$a = (7 + 9) \div (9 - 5)$$
$$b = 7 + 9 \div 9 - 5$$

Evaluate $a \times b$.

A. 2
B. 4
C. 9
D. 12
E. 16

70.

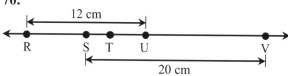

In the number line above, RS = SU and TU = 2(ST). What is TU – ST + UV?

F. 4
G. 8
H. 10
J. 14
K. 16

71. Nate rolls a fair, six-sided die 5 times. What is the probability that he will get at least 2 evens?

A. $\dfrac{1}{32}$

B. $\dfrac{3}{32}$

C. $\dfrac{3}{16}$

D. $\dfrac{19}{32}$

E. $\dfrac{13}{16}$

CONTINUE ▶

72. Margot drove 450 miles to a resort at an average speed of 50 miles per hour. She later drove back at an average speed of 60 miles per hour. What was her average speed for the entire trip (rounded to the nearest hundredth)?

    F. 27.27 miles per hour
    G. 28.28 miles per hour
    H. 54.54 miles per hour
    J. 55.00 miles per hour
    K. 56.56 miles per hour

73. Angles X and Y are supplementary. Angles X and Z are complementary. Based on this information, which of the following **must** be true?

    A. Y is an obtuse angle.
    B. Y and Z are complementary.
    C. $Y - X = Z$
    D. The measure of X is greater than that of Z.
    E. Y and Z are supplementary.

74. What is the sum of 25% of 16 and 16% of 25?

    F. 50% of 16
    G. 41% of 25
    H. 41% of 16
    J. 9% of 9
    K. 141% of 41

75. Lenny and Teddy have between them $7.75 in quarters and dimes. Lenny has twice as many quarters as Teddy does, but Teddy has 4 times as many dimes as Lenny does. How many quarters does Lenny have if he has 2 dimes?

    A. 16
    B. 17
    C. 18
    D. 19
    E. 20

76.

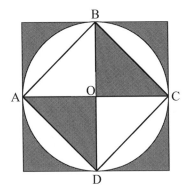

Circle O, which is inscribed in a square, in turn has a square inscribed within it. If the area of circle O is 16π in², what is the area of the shaded region?

    F. $80 - 16\pi$ in²
    G. $72 - 16\pi$ in²
    H. $68 - 20\pi$ in²
    J. $64 - 16\pi$ in²
    K. $64 - 8\pi$ in²

77. If $\dfrac{7r - 2p}{5} = 8p$, what is the value of $3r^2$?

    A. $18p^2$
    B. $36p^2$
    C. $98p^2$
    D. $108p^2$
    E. $126p^2$

78. Wilfred placed a sticky note on every third page of his notebook, starting page 1. That is, he placed sticky notes on pages 1, 4, 7, and so on. If there are 300 pages in his notebook, how many sticky notes did he place?

    F. 97
    G. 98
    H. 99
    J. 100
    K. 101

CONTINUE ▶

79.

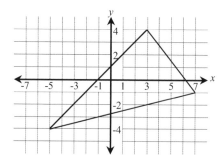

What is the area of the triangle in the coordinate plane above, in units squared?

A. 24
B. 36
C. 48
D. 60
E. 96

80. What is 1.56×10^7 divided by 1.95×10^6?

F. 4
G. 8
H. 16
J. 40
K. 80

81. If a cargo jet can hold exactly 79 boats in weight, and 2 boats weigh the same as 3 cars, how many whole cars can the cargo jet hold at most? Assume space doesn't matter.

A. 52
B. 53
C. 104
D. 118
E. 119

82. What is the surface area of a box whose edges measure 6 inches, 13 inches, and 5 inches?

F. 65 sq in
G. 78 sq in
H. 143 sq in
J. 173 sq in
K. 346 sq in

83. Emil is 43 years old currently. 9 years ago, he was twice the age of Roderick. How old will Roderick be in 15 years from now?

A. 17
B. 29
C. 32
D. 34
E. 41

84. If the ratio of the amount of homework Martin has left to do to the amount he has completed is 2 to 7, approximately what percent of his homework did he complete?

F. 11
G. 22
H. 29
J. 78
K. 89

85. A bobcat is tethered by a 24-foot chain to a vertex inside of a regular hexagonal cage whose sides are 30 feet each. How much area does the bobcat have access to? (The interior angles of a regular hexagon all add to 720°.)

A. 96π sq ft
B. 128π sq ft
C. 192π sq ft
D. 288π sq ft
E. 384π sq ft

86. In a town of 12,000, 63% of the residents support Plan A. If 74% support Plan B, and everyone supports at least one of the plans, how many people support both?

F. 1,320
G. 2,220
H. 2,640
J. 3,960
K. 4,440

CONTINUE ▶

87.

Ms. Kim's Drama Students

Student	Age	Height (in.)
Avery	13	60
Chauncey	11	53
Emmitt	10	54
Josefina	12	63
Dewey	12	58
Wallace	11	57
Victor	10	53

Which student best represents the average height and age of Mrs. Kim's drama class?

A. Chauncey
B. Wallace
C. Dewey
D. Josefina
E. Avery

---

88. Let $\text{✦x✦} = \dfrac{1}{x} \times \dfrac{x+3}{2}$. For what value of x does $\text{✦x✦} = 5$?

F. $\dfrac{1}{5}$

G. $\dfrac{1}{3}$

H. $\dfrac{1}{2}$

J. 3

K. 5

---

89. An audience of between 2,400 and 2,500 is being split into groups of 6. If 3 people are left over without a group, what is the greatest number of people that can be in the audience?

A. 2,500
B. 2,499
C. 2,498
D. 2,497
E. 2,493

---

90. If the coordinates (3, 0) and (6, 4) represent two adjacent vertices of a square, what is the area of the square, in units squared?

F. 49
G. 36
H. 25
J. 20
K. 16

91.

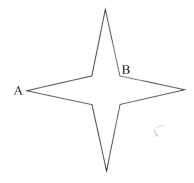

It takes Al 24 minutes to run the above course without retracing his steps. Each segment is equal in length. How many **seconds** would have elapsed by the time Al makes it to point B for the tenth time, when he starts from point A and runs clockwise around the course?

A. 14,940
B. 13,500
C. 7,470
D. 6,750
E. 225

---

92. If there are 3,987 cars in a city of 31,867 people, what is the best estimate of the ratio of cars to people?

F. 1:8
G. 3:8
H. 1:4
J. 3:16
K. 4:31

CONTINUE ▶

93. Otis walks 3 blocks east from his house and then 5 blocks north to get to his friend's house. From his friend's house, 7 blocks south and 7 blocks west to get to an arcade. After Otis goes back home from the arcade, how many total blocks will he have walked, since initially starting out from his house?

    A. 28
    B. 22
    C. 17
    D. 14
    E. 6

94. According to a certain scale diagram, Neal's backyard should extend 35 yards by 40 yards. If, on the diagram, his backyard was drawn 14 inches by 16 inches, what is the scale that was used?

    F. 1:128
    G. 1:90
    H. 1:64
    J. 1:45
    K. 1:2.5

95.

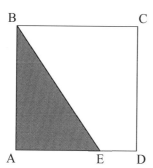

What is the perimeter of trapezoid BEDC, if the area of square ABCD is 225 cm^2 and the ratio of AE to ED is 2:1?

    A. 42 cm
    B. $5(7 + 2\sqrt{2})$ cm
    C. $5(7 + 2\sqrt{3})$ cm
    D. $5(7 + \sqrt{13})$ cm
    E. $40\sqrt{13}$ cm

96. If a rectangular photograph is increased by 400% on each side, what percent of the area of the original is the enlarged photograph?

    F. 400%
    G. 800%
    H. 1,600%
    J. 2,000%
    K. 2,500%

97. In a survey conducted by a department store, it was shown that 3 out of 8 shoppers were male. If there was a total of 608 shoppers, how many more female shoppers were there than male shoppers?

    A. 364
    B. 304
    C. 228
    D. 179
    E. 152

98. What is the value of $(2x - 3y)(3y + 2x)$ if $x = 11$ and $y = 10$?

    F. ⁻416
    G. ⁻208
    H. 0
    J. 208
    K. 416

99.

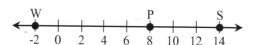

On the number line above, what is the value of PS ÷ WP?

    A. 16
    B. 2
    C. 0.6
    D. 0.67
    E. 0.33

CONTINUE ▶

100.

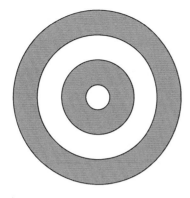

The target above was made using four circles. The radii of the circles are respectively 1, 3, 5, and 7 inches. If an arrow hits the target randomly, what is the probability that it will hit a shaded region of the target?

F. $\dfrac{1}{2}$

G. $\dfrac{2}{3}$

H. $\dfrac{31}{49}$

J. $\dfrac{32}{49}$

K. $\dfrac{36}{49}$

STOP. THIS IS THE END OF THE TEST. IF TIME PERMITS, YOU MAY REVIEW YOUR ANSWERS TO PARTS 1 AND 2 OF THE TEST.

ANSWERS
& EXPLANATIONS

SHSAT
TJHSST EDITION
TEST KEY 1

AK

Answer Key – Test 1

VERBAL

SCRAMBLED PARAGRAPHS

Paragraph 1
USRQT

Paragraph 2
TRSQU

Paragraph 3
QTSRU

Paragraph 4
SURTQ

Paragraph 5
TURSQ

LOGICAL REASONING

11. A
12. J
13. D
14. G
15. E
16. J
17. C
18. G
19. C
20. G
21. B
22. K
23. A
24. J
25. D

READING

26. J
27. D
28. J
29. D
30. G
31. E
32. G
33. A
34. H
35. C
36. G
37. D
38. K
39. D
40. F
41. B
42. H
43. D
44. G
45. C
46. G
47. A
48. G
49. B
50. J

MATH ANSWERS ▶

Answer Key – Test 1

MATHEMATICS

51.	E		76.	J
52.	K		77.	C
53.	D		78.	H
54.	F		79.	A
55.	C		80.	G
56.	G		81.	D
57.	A		82.	H
58.	K		83.	B
59.	B		84.	K
60.	J		85.	D
61.	C		86.	H
62.	H		87.	A
63.	C		88.	K
64.	F		89.	A
65.	D		90.	J
66.	J		91.	A
67.	E		92.	H
68.	G		93.	C
69.	A		94.	J
70.	K		95.	B
71.	D		96.	F
72.	J		97.	B
73.	E		98.	J
74.	G		99.	A
75.	E		100.	K

VERBAL EXPLANATIONS ▶

Answer Explanations – Verbal
Practice Test 1

SCRAMBLED PARAGRAPHS

Paragraph 1 (USRQT)

The opening sentence mentions that some animals defy easy classification. Sentence U introduces the platypus as an animal that does defy easy classification. The rest of the paragraph will thus focus on the platypus.

It may not be an easy task to identify which sentence comes after sentence U, so it is important to use some logical reasoning to determine the next sentence.

By reading the other sentences, it becomes clear that R follows S, for a couple of reasons. S states that it might be easy to conclude from looking at the platypus's bill and webbed feed that the platypus belongs to the class of birds. R adds on to S by stating that the platypus does not permit such easy conclusions. In other words, the phrase "easy conclusions" in R serves as a transition from "easy to conclude" in S.

Following R, which introduces the fact that the platypus has a largely mammalian body, is Q. Q states that despite the platypus's largely mammalian bodies, there are still yet some other oddities that make it hard to pinpoint the platypus's classification, in particular pointing out that the female platypus lays eggs and that the male has stingers.

Note: Both S and Q indicate traits that make it difficult to conclude that the platypus is mammal, but the phrase "even more bizarre" indicates that sentence Q comes sometime after sentence S, if it was not obvious already, from the explanation thus far, that Q comes after S.

Finally, T is last because it concludes that the platypus is indeed mammal. It introduces the final points that define what mammals are.

The above explanation leads to the order SRQT after U, which means that the correct arrangement of the paragraph after the lead sentence is USRQT.

Paragraph 2 (TRSQU)

The lead sentence calls to attention Thomas Edison's prominence as one of the most prolific inventors in history, setting up the rest of the paragraph to be about Edison. It should be quickly noticed, however, that the remainder of the sentences are not about Edison directly.

Sentence T follows the lead because it introduces Edwin Barnes and provides a transition from the lead sentence by stating that Edwin Barnes is not as well-known as Edison is. R follows T because it establishes a contrast to T's mention of Barnes's success as Edison's business associate and it sets up the rest of the paragraph to discuss Barnes's rise to success. After R, which depicts the extent of Barnes's poverty, comes S, which describes how Barnes was able to get arrive at Edison's business headquarters. Q then comes after S because it mentions Barnes's actual arrival at Edison's workplace. U wraps the paragraph up by indicating that Barnes's hard work and dedication paid off in the end.

Note: It may be tempting to select sentence U before sentence Q. Sentence U refers to the great lengths to which Barnes went in order to work with Edison, and sentence S discusses burning all bridges behind him, which most would agree is drastic and qualifies as great lengths. If U is picked before Q, however, that would make Q the conclusion, but it doesn't make sense to say that Barnes's efforts paid out in the end and then have Barnes work for years as a janitor before any semblance of opportunity presented itself.

Paragraph 3 (QTSRU)

The lead sentence calls to attention the entrenchment of video games in society. Sentence Q follows the lead because it elaborates on how entrenched, or rooted, video games have become; it states that the video game industry is worth $60.4 billion in 2009.

T follows Q because it refers to the multibillion dollar status of the video game industry and sets the tone for a brief overview of the history of video games. S follows T by introducing the first video game to be created in 1952. R therefore naturally follows S since the events it describes occurs two decades later, in 1972. U concludes the paragraph with its discussion of video games in present day.

Hint: This scrambled paragraph was one based on chronology, so figuring out the dates and timeframes will greatly aid in establishing the order of the sentences. Establish clusters with TSR. Then it should be apparent that U comes after R and Q comes before T as the sentence after the lead sentence.

Paragraph 4 (SURTQ)

The opening sentence compares the internet of today and the internet as it was in its infancy. Sentence S follows the lead because it explains how telephony was used to connect to the internet.

U comes after S because S mentions that internet access was achieved by using telephony to transmit packets of data, and U explains how the transmission of data over phone lines opened up many opportunities while minimizing our dependence on traditional methods of communication. R establishes what types of traditional methods of communication were minimized and what forms of communications opportunities the internet provided.

T then follows R with "with such diverse communication avenues now available" and further elaborates on R.

Note: T may seem like a good alternative to R, as the sentence that comes after U, with R expounding on what T states. Pay close attention to the details, though. R is the better choice because it explains what traditional methods of communication are being less depended on; T does not offer such a connection to U. Furthermore, the phrase "*such diverse communication avenues*" indicates a specification of communication avenues, but the opportunities and communication methods mentioned in U are too broadly stated to properly satisfy a strong connection to T.

Q concludes the paragraph with a discussion of the impact of broadband internet, bringing the paragraph full circle back to the lead sentence.

Paragraph 5 (TURSQ)

The introductory sentence of the paragraph introduces Francis Scott Key, his poem "Defence of Fort McHenry," and his desire to make a song out of the poem.

Sentence T comes after the introductory sentence because it refers to Key's intended song and the likelihood that he could not have anticipated the grandiose fate of his song. U comes after T because it explains how, indeed, the fate of Key's poem was more the product of luck than planning.

R begins to explain the circumstances under which the American national anthem was created. Key, an attorney and poet, had boarded a British vessel. S comes after R because it explains why Key boarded. And Q, the conclusion, explains what exactly had prompted Key to write the poem that would eventually become the national anthem.

Hint: Make a two-sentence cluster out of TU, as those sentences are clearly linked. Then establish a cluster of RSQ because those sentences discuss the circumstances that led to Key's writing of the poem. At this point, it should become deducible that either T or R will be the sentence to follow the lead, and it makes more sense for T to precede U.

LOGICAL REASONING ▶

AE

LOGICAL REASONING

11. **(A)** From the information given, it is possible to conclude that Daniel's house is also smaller than Richard's house. It is also possible to conclude that all of the houses in Ashville are smaller than James's house, which is the correct answer.

    B and C are not correct because not enough information has been given as to the comparative sizes of the houses of Ashville and the size of Daniel's house.

    D and E are not correct because, again, not enough information has been given. While both Daniel's house and the houses of Ashville are smaller than James's and Richard's houses, there is no valid basis for concluding that Daniel's house is in or is not in Ashville. It is possible that Daniel's house is in Ashville and equally possible that Daniel's house is not in Ashville.

12. **(J)** The only possible conclusion that can be drawn from the facts is that Ray is not the fastest swimmer on Team USA. There is no mention of the swimmers' sizes, which rules out choice F; similarly, there is no connection between swimming speed and the number of pizzas a swimmer can eat in a sitting, which rules out H.

    The facts do not indicate whether Ray is a swimmer on Team USA or not, so choices G and K are ruled out. This leaves J as the correct choice.

13. **(D)** Three of Jamal's pets eat the same type of food, which means he keeps a total of two extra bags of food for those three pets. The other four pets do not share food, meaning that there are two extra bags of pet food for each of those four pets, for a total of eight extra bags of food for those four. Adding two (from the three pets that share food) and eight yields ten extra bags of food that Jamal must keep, if he is to follow his rule.

14. **(G)** This question tests logic statements. To find the correct answer, it is necessary to determine the contrapositives of the two conditional statements.

    First, assume that the conditional statements are true. The contrapositives of the conditional statements are as follows: 1) If I go to school, then it is not snowing heavily, and 2) If I go to school, then it is not a holiday. Since both contrapositives apply in this case, the correct choice is G.

15. **(E)** To solve this problem, draw a diagram or chart that will illustrate the order in which Kathy passed the six automobiles. First, draw the diagram in with Fiat as the last one Kathy passed and the BMW as the third one she passed.

    Because Kathy passed the Lexus after she passed the Dodge and Chevrolet, the Lexus has to be either the fourth or fifth car she passed. But when it is further considered that Kathy passed the Lexus before she passed the Hyundai, it becomes apparent that the Lexus must be the fourth car that Kathy passed, and the Hyundai is the fifth.

	First Passed
1.	Dodge/Chevrolet
2.	Dodge/Chevrolet
3.	BMW
4.	Lexus
5.	Hyundai
6.	Fiat
	Last Passed

This leaves the Dodge and Chevrolet as the first two cars Kathy passed. Since the Dodge was not the first car that Kathy passed, however, the Dodge must be the second and the Chevrolet the first cars that Kathy passed. Therefore, E lists the correct order in which Kathy passed the six automobiles.

16. (J) There is not enough information provided to definitively establish an order of distances the football was thrown. Therefore, F and K can be eliminated from the outset.

G is not correct. Even if Patrick threw the ball the farthest, it is not necessarily the case that Simon threw the ball the second farthest. It is feasible that Simon threw the ball third farthest or least far. Note, the question is asking for which of the following must be true. H is incorrect for a similar reason. If Quentin threw the ball the farthest, it is still feasible for Timothy to have thrown the ball the second farthest.

This leaves J as the correct answer. If Simon threw the ball farther than Timothy did, then either Quentin or Patrick threw the ball the farthest. Remember that Simon could not have thrown the ball the farthest, since Patrick threw farther than Simon did. This leaves either Patrick or Quentin as the only options for the farthest thrower.

Hint: When dealing with "must be true" questions, even one counterexample that disproves an answer choice rules that choice out.

17. (C) Draw a diagram to solve this problem by filling in as much information as possible. It does not matter in this case where you begin to fill the information in, as this problem is about relative and not absolute positions.

Once you fill in what you can from the information presented and from the question itself, you should have something similar to the following diagram:

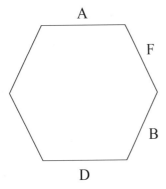

Note: Keep in mind that the students are facing the table. In order to figure out the lefts and rights of the students, you have to do it from the perspectives of the students as they are facing the table. In other words, if Frank were placed on the other side of Alice in the diagram, he would be to *her* right, even though he would be to the left of her in the diagram itself.

Once the above diagram is drawn, it becomes obvious that only four students were mentioned. Looking at the answer choices should quickly supply the remaining name: Carter.

Since Dylan is not sitting next to the empty space, Carter should be placed in the empty spot next to Dylan. Once Carter is placed, the order of the students becomes complete, and the correct answer becomes obvious.

Only choices A and C have Alice to the left of the empty spot. Dylan comes before Carter, when starting from the empty seat and going to its left, so the correct choice is C.

18. (G) Because Mawsynram is, on average, the wettest place in the world, all other places receive less rainfall than Mawsynram does, which means that they receive an average of less than 474.4 inches of rainfall per year.

F is incorrect because it presumes that the Atacama Desert is the driest place in the world. From the numbers alone, it may certainly seem like that's true, but it is not possible to infer from the passage that this is actually the case. Similarly, there is not enough information to support J as the correct choice.

H and K are incorrect for similar reasons. H is wrong because, while it might seem obvious that the Atacama Desert always receives less rain in any given month than Mawsynram does in the same month, this conclusion is not supported by the passage. For instance, it is possible for Mawsynram to receive no rain in one month while the Atacama Desert receives an inch of rain that month. The same logic applies to rule K out.

19. **(C)** Here, the best strategy is to also draw a diagram or chart. But keep in mind that there are two things to keep track of: students and colors.

First Place

1.	– Red
2.	Justin – Orange
3.	– Yellow
4.	Kylie – Blue
5.	Harold – Green

Last Place

From the numbered clues, the above chart can be constructed. The question itself provides the last pieces we need to fill out the entire diagram. Lisa comes after Irene, which makes Irene, on the red team, first place and Lisa, on the yellow team, third place.

20. **(G)** There are two ways to solve this problem. One way is to draw a diagram.

	1	2	3	4	5	6	7	8	9	1 0
T	X	X					X	X	X	
F	X	X	X	X	X	X	X			
G			X	X	X	X		X		

As the chart above shows, it is possible to have Clarisse play 17 seasons of sports in 9 years.

Another way to think about this problem is to divide 17 by 2, since Clarisse is playing two sports per year. That yields 8 with a remainder of 1. The remainder of 1 represents the ninth year.

Note: Beware of the diagramming method. It is very easy to get 10 or 12 years, but those do not represent the fewest number of years Clarisse would need to play 17 seasons of sports.

21. **(B)** Draw out a chart or diagram.

Before drawing out a diagram, however, it may be helpful to draw some logical conclusions.

First, we can conclude that Xavier has the purple lunchbox because the facts indicate that Zack, Yolanda, and Wendy all do not have the purple lunchbox. This means that Zack stood directly behind Xavier in line.

And since Xavier is behind Yolanda but ahead of Wendy, Yolanda is first in line and Xavier is second in line. Since Zack is directly behind Xavier, that means he is third in line, thereby putting Wendy last in line.

Now that the order of the students has been determined, the following diagram or chart can be drawn:

First in Line

1.	Yolanda –
2.	Xavier – Purple
3.	Zack –
4.	Wendy –

Last in Line

And looking at the last clue, it is possible to ascertain that the turquoise lunchbox is last and the lavender lunchbox first, with the burgundy lunchbox in between them. This would mean that the burgundy lunchbox belongs to Zack.

22. **(K)** The problem mentions three sports: wrestling, American football, and soccer. Paul participates in two of these sports. The most logical conclusion is that Paul must play American football, which rules out choice H. Unfortunately, that's not an available answer choice, so it is necessary to look through the possibilities.

Paul's two options are either he plays American football and wrestles or he plays both American football and soccer. This rules choices F and G out because it possible for Paul to play American football without wrestling and for him to play American football without also playing soccer. If he plays soccer, he cannot also wrestle, as that would indicate that he plays three sports, since all wrestlers also play American football in this problem. This rules out J. Our only remaining choice is K, the correct choice: if Paul plays soccer, then he does not also wrestle.

Logic Note: Just because every wrestler also plays American football does not necessarily mean that every American football player also wrestles.

23. **(A)** To solve this problem, the various initiatives and procedures Neil takes or applies should be mapped out.

To start, if Neil receives response M, then he will take initiative A. If A succeeds, he will take initiative K and he won't take initiative X.

If initiative A fails, then Neil will take initiative X. If X succeeds, then Neil will take initiative K. If X fails, however, then Neil applies procedure Y.

It is thus possible to see that there are only two possible outcomes to Neil's actions, whenever he receives response M from a prospective employer: initiative K or procedure Y.

If Neil took neither initiative X nor applied procedure Y, Neil took initiatives A and K. Neil takes initiative X only if A fails, but A didn't fail, which means A succeeded. And if A succeeded, Neil took initiative K, which is represented by answer choice A.

B is incorrect because there is not enough information to determine whether initiative K failed or succeeded. D is wrong for similar reasons; there is not enough information to make the conclusion stated in D.

C is incorrect because it is contradicts the fourth numbered statement of fact, and E is incorrect because there is enough information to arrive at choice A.

24. **(J)** To solve problems such as this, it is important to see which words and corresponding letters overlap among the sentences. In this way, it is possible to narrow down or deduce which letters are assigned to which words.

To determine which letter means "house," it is first important to realize that "house" only appears in the second and fourth sentences. The second and fourth sentences have three words in common: "walked," "to," and "house." Furthermore, the coded versions of the second and fourth sentences share the letters Z, Y, and M, meaning that these letters are the only possible choices to represent the three words.

But before continuing, it must also be realized that the words "walked" and "to" are used in every sentence. Similarly, the letters Z and Y appear in every coded sentence. This means that the letters Z and Y represent the words "walked" and "to," although it is impossible to specifically identify which letter is assigned to which word.

With Z and Y meaning "walked" and "to," M is left to mean "house." Thus, choice J is correct.

25. **(D)** To solve this problem, it is important to figure out, at least to the extent deductions will permit, which letters unequivocally represent which words.

Question 24 revealed that "house" is represented by M. It is also possible to see that the first and third sentences share the word "the" and the letter W. This is the extent of the deductions that are permitted, indicating that the letters K, W, A, Y, Q, S, B, and P cannot be conclusively assigned. Additionally, from Question 24, it was determined that Z and Y cannot be definitively assigned, as well. Altogether, this amounts to 10 letters that can be assigned to more than one word.

READING ▶

AE

READING

(Rosa Parks)

26. (J) This passages discusses why Rosa Parks refused to give up her seat and the lasting legacy of her refusal. By going through a process of elimination, it is possible to see why J is the correct choice.

F may seem appealing, as a generally accurate statement, but it is too far removed from this passage; it is off-topic. G is incorrect. While the Montgomery Bus Boycott fueled other boycotts and helped the civil rights movement achieve its agenda, it cannot be concluded that the Montgomery Bus Boycott was necessary for civil rights movements. It is possible that civil rights movements could have succeeded without it. This choice is too presumptuous.

H is a correct statement, but it is too narrow in scope. Rosa Parks's refusal to give up her seat because she was tired of giving in is one aspect of the passage, but not even close to the majority of it. K is incorrect because it is unsupported by the passage. Nothing indicates that Rosa Parks was the greatest civil rights activist ever.

27. (D) The third paragraph (lines 18-26) answers this question directly. Rosa Parks's arrest sparked a problem that required a delicate solution, and this solution was a boycott. Lines 22-24, in particular, state that the black men and women were to boycott the buses.

28. (J) Lines 3-4 state that the buses had rows reserved for black bus patrons. Lines 5-8 show that Rosa Parks and others were expected to move to other seats to accommodate incoming white passengers. The second paragraph (lines 9-17) indicate that it was the law for black patrons to make room for white ones when not enough seating was available for the white passengers. Lines 25-26 imply that some of the rows of the buses were dedicated to black passengers only, specifically the rows in the back of the buses. These facts support choice J.

F is incorrect because it is stated in the passage that the front of the bus was reserved for white passengers exclusively. G may be tempting, but lines 25-26 imply that black passengers could only be asked to move from middle rows, if the front rows filled up.

H is incorrect because it draws too strong of a conclusion. It is not discussed in the article whether passengers of other ethnicities were also allowed to sit in the back rows. K is incorrect because it goes directly against what is stated in lines 25-26. One of the reasons the boycott took place was precisely that the middle rows weren't available to all patrons on a "first come, first serve" basis.

29. (D) Lines 22-25 indicate that the boycott would persist until several demands were met, and one of those demands was for the city to hire black drivers. Thus, D is correct.

A is incorrect because lines 14-16 state that Rosa Parks refused to give up her seat because she didn't see why she had to and that she was tired of giving in. B is incorrect because it is not supported by the passage. The passage does not mention that Rosa Parks's last name was McCauley at one point. C is incorrect because it is too presumptuous. It is certainly possible that Martin Luther King, Jr. could have risen to prominence without Rosa Parks. E may be a tempting choice, but it is one thing to say the city probably lost a lot of money because of the boycott and another to say the city's bus system "would have made a fortune" if the boycott hadn't occurred.

30. (G) Rosa Parks's refusal to give up her seat led to her arrest, and her arrest consequently led to the Montgomery Bus Boycott because her arrest required a delicate solution that would maintain peace in the community; the boycott was the proposed solution.

F and H, and F in particular, are traps. They are tempting because they appeal strongly to common sense. The problem, however, is that neither is supported by the passage. In the case of F, the Supreme Court ruled on the constitutionality of segregation on buses as a result of the Montgomery Bus Boycott (fourth paragraph, lines 27-34). Nothing is mentioned in the passage about how the Supreme Court would have eventually deemed segregation unconstitutional. In the case of G, the passage mentions in lines 39-42 that the Montgomery Bus Boycott "provided the springboard for Martin Luther King, Jr. to vault in the national spotlight and serve as a champion of nonviolent protest and reform." Nowhere in the passage does it indicate that Martin Luther King, Jr. would have achieved the same level of prominence regardless.

J is incorrect. In lines 28-34, the passage states that 381 days, or more than a year, elapsed between Rosa Parks's arrest and the Supreme Court's decision to rule that Alabama's segregation laws for buses were unconstitutional. K is incorrect because the bus driver presumably did call the police, which is how Rosa Parks was arrested—line 11 of the passage mentions that the bus driver threatened to call the police.

(*Animal Farm*)

31. **(E)** The purpose of *Animal Farm* can best be represented by E. The first paragraph (lines 1-4) tells what George Orwell tried to accomplish by writing *Animal Farm*.

    A, C, and D may be true statements, but they are not the primary reasons George Orwell wrote *Animal Farm*. The passage discusses the transformation of the pigs and the corruption that befalls them. B is completely unsupported or unsubstantiated by the passage.

32. **(G)** Lines 23-29 show that Animalism was meant to promote equality among animals and that they were supposed to revile humans. Therefore, G is correct. The other options are not supported by the passage.

33. **(A)** The only choice that is not mentioned as a contributing factor to the animals' rebellion against Mr. Jones is option A. The passage neither state nor even implies that the pigs had a desire to rule the world.

    B and D are incorrect because it is mentioned in lines 16-20 that Mr. Jones's neglectfulness and the animals' growing discontentment were contributing factors to the rebellion. C is also incorrect because Mr. Jones's whipping of the animals, mentioned in lines 20-22, probably contributed to the rebellion. E is incorrect because Old Major's dream (lines 5-13) was precisely what prompted the animals to prepare for a rebellion to begin with.

34. **(H)** It can be inferred that Napoleon had been planning Snowball's exile for some time because he trained the dogs secretly for years.

    F is incorrect because there is no mention of the dogs having been trained by police officers. G may be appealing because Squealer reveals that Snowball had been plotting treachery against Animal Farm all along, but two things make this choice incorrect. First, lines 40-43 show that Squealer and Napoleon were trying to convince the other animals that Snowball had been plotting treachery; it is not established that Snowball actually had been doing so. Second, H says Snowball had been planning to destroy Animal Farm, which is not necessarily the same as plotting pernicious treachery.

    J is incorrect; there was no voting process; the animals also did not learn of Snowballs alleged treachery until after he was driven out. K is incorrect because it is not mentioned or hinted at anywhere in the passage that Snowball had left to spread Animalism.

35. **(C)** Choice C is supported by the last paragraph in lines 44-49.

    A is incorrect because the pigs violate the Seven Commandments as they please, as evidenced by lines 44-49. B is incorrect because it is unsupported by the passage; there is no mention of the Bible's Ten Commandments. D is incorrect because it draws a faulty conclusion—if anything, if the Seven Commandments hadn't existed, then the pigs would have obtained absolute power more quickly. E is incorrect because Old Major's involvement in the creation of the Seven Commandments is not mentioned or hinted at.

(Paralympics)

36. **(G)** The passage was intended to provide some context for the Paralympic Games, touching on the history of the Games and the impact they've had on the world and on the athletes who compete in them. The other choices are incorrect because they are too narrow in focus.

37. **(D)** D is correct because the author is reporting facts about the Paralympic Games and several of the participants. But it is also apparent that the author has great respect for the athletes, particularly in lines 11-21. The other options have at least one erroneous part.

38. **(K)** The last paragraph, from lines 37-43, show that the author believes that the Paralympic Games will continue to be of greater global significance in the future.

F is incorrect. Just because the 2012 Games outsold the 2008 Games by 900,000 does not mean the 2016 Games will outsell the 2012 Games by the same margin. G is incorrect because it is worded too strongly. While it would certainly be an ideal that the Paralympic Games would like to achieve, not everyone will embrace the visions and values of the Paralympics.

H is incorrect because it is not supported that every future Paralympics Games will outsell the 2012 London Games. While it is true that the author expects the global influence of the Paralympics Games to increase in the future, this does not mean the author expects every Paralympics Games to outsell the 2012 London Games. J is incorrect; there is no mention

in the passage about the comparability of athletes' courage and determination.

39. **(D)** In lines 31-36, it is stated that the audience turnout and ticket sales for the 2012 Games reached unprecedented levels. This implies that the Games had not been as successful in the past. D is therefore correct.

A is not implied by the passage, even though it might seem logical or reasonable, given that the 2008 Beijing Games were directly compared to the London Games. Based on the information presented in the passage, however, it is not possible to know if the Games had previously surpassed the Beijing Games in terms of sales and audience turnout. B is too strong of a statement. Lieutenant Snyder was probably one of the best swimmers of the Paralympic Games, given that he won multiple medals and set a record for the 100-meter freestyle event (lines 3-7), but that does not mean he was the Games' best athlete. E is not supported by the passage. The passage states in lines 16-21 that thousands of athletes have epitomized the values of the Paralympics. It does not state that every Paralympics athlete has been honorable and inspirational role models. The possibility of dishonesty and dishonorableness is left open.

40. **(F)** The values of the Paralympic Games are stated in lines 19-20: courage, determination, inspiration, and equality. Thus, excellence is not one of those values, even though it is a part of the vision of the Paralympic Games, as stated in the quote in lines 25-27. The other choices are stated values of the Paralympic Games.

(Statue of Liberty)

41. **(B)** This passage is about the Statue of Liberty's conception and construction and one of the obstacles that nearly prevented the statue's completion. B captures this accurately. The other choices are incorrect because they focus too narrowly on snippets of the passage.

42. (H) The Statue of Liberty was originally planned to be delivered to the United States in 1876 as a centennial gift (lines 10-14). This means that the American Declaration of Independence was adopted in 1776.

43. (D) In lines 35-39, it is stated that by the time the pedestal was completed, the Statue had already arrived in New York Harbor, awaiting assembly. If the pedestal had been completed before the Statue arrived from France, then the Statue could have been assembled earlier. D represents this conclusion accurately.

A and E are wrong because they state or assume that the Statue's assembly was completed in October 1886. In lines 36-41, it is stated that the pedestal was completed in April 1886 and that assembly of the Statue took four months. Four months after April is August, which is more than a month removed from October. Thus, even if assembly of the Statue began in May, it would have been completed sometime in September at the latest. There is, of course, a certain degree of ambiguity as to the word "immediately" (line 40), but this ambiguity could go either way. It could mean the Statue's assembly began sometime in April or May or that assembly began in June, perhaps. But because there is this ambiguity, it is cannot be assumed that assembly began later rather than sooner.

B is incorrect because the passage makes no mentions of inclement weather conditions. C is incorrect because it is not revealed by the passage when the Statue arrived in New York Harbor. If the Statue did not arrive in New York Harbor until after August 1885, then C would not work. As it stands, there is not enough information to support choice C.

44. (G) Lines 30-34 indicate that it took six months to raise $100,000 and that financing for the pedestal was completed in August 1885. Six months prior to August is February, so G is correct.

None of the other options are supported or stated by the passage. H and K, in particular, are appealing because they focus on the fact that the average contribution per person was less than one dollar. This does not mean, however, that no one donated over two dollars. Furthermore, just because the average donation was under a dollar does not mean that most of the people donating were mean and stingy. It is possible that most of the contributors could not afford to give a dollar or more, as money was worth more then.

45. (C) This question was designed to be extremely tricky. All of the answer choices, especially A, have legitimate arguments in favor of them. If you notice carefully, however, the question asks, "Whom would the *author* probably credit...?" In lines 44-46, the author writes that the Statue was thankfully seen to the end by the dedicated people of America and France. And, certainly, such people as Joseph Pulitzer would be considered among "people of America and France." Thus, C is the best answer.

(Asthma)

46. (G) The best choice is G. The passage encourages taking preventive action in lines 19-26, 27-33, and 51-53. The other choices, whose contents are mentioned in the passage to some extent, are too narrowly focused to be the main purpose of the passage.

47. (A) The passage implies that children's lungs are more susceptible to long-term damage. Lines 27-33 state that it is important to detect the triggers of and prevent asthma in children because their lungs are still underdeveloped. They also state that early detection and prevention can ensure a more enjoyable childhood and healthier adulthood, indicating children's underdeveloped lungs are more prone to long-term damage than adults' are.

B is incorrect; the passage does not state that all molds cause children to develop asthma. C is incorrect because the passage states in lines

19-21 that genetic preventive measures against asthma are not possible. D is incorrect. Lines 31-33 state that "early detection and prevention can ensure a more enjoyable childhood and healthier adulthood." This does not mean that the passage is suggesting or stating that children with asthma grow up to become unhappy adults. E is incorrect because it is not mentioned in the passage at all. Be careful of the age reference; it was inserted into choice E as a trap. Lines 43-45 mention the age 7, but the age is not linked to the prevention of adult asthma.

48. **(G)** Lines 3-9 describe asthma and what happens to cause its various symptoms. The best answer choice is G; if the airways are becoming swollen and filled with mucous, the size of the openings of the airways is going to be smaller than normal. With less air able to pass through his or her airways, the asthmatic will experience a shortness of breath and its various manifestations.

F is inviting, but beware of choices such as this one. It is incorrect because the soreness by itself isn't responsible for asthmatics' inability to breathe properly when they experience an asthma attack. H might sound like a good choice because it is vaguely worded, but this is also a red herring. It is incorrect because the symptoms are not what cause breathing difficulties; the breathing difficulties, such as coughing, shortness of breath, and wheezing, are the symptoms of asthma.

J is only partially accurate because the passage does not say that mucous completely blocks the passage of air into the lungs, even though the passage does mention in line 7 that mucous fills up the airways. K is inaccurate, as well. The passage does not state that asthma always leads to critical damage to internal organs. The passage does say in lines 9-12 is that if the asthma attack is severe enough, it *may* damage internal organs.

49. **(B)** Lines 48-50 suggest that home owners should consider remediating their homes for mold problems, which aligns with choice B.

A is incorrect because it is too strong of an assertion. While three species of mold have been most commonly associated with asthma (lines 45-48), this does not necessarily mean that they are the only species that have any effect on the development of asthma. C is incorrect; it is never stated or suggested in the passage that asthma is the leading cause of death among respiratory diseases and illnesses. The only discussion of the extent of asthma's reach is in lines 1-2, which indicate that asthma is a nontrivial global issue. D is incorrect. Lines 14-17 indicate asthma can be influenced by genetics as well as the environment. E is incorrect; it is never suggested or stated in the passage that surgical masks should be worn to prevent any triggers from entering into asthmatics' airways. Furthermore, the author never suggests that people suffering from asthma should take drastic measures to prevent encounters with any possible trigger.

50. **(J)** The best answer is J. If an asthma trigger is not obvious, then the chances decrease that the asthmatic knows that the trigger is a trigger. If the asthmatic does not know that something is a trigger, he or she will not think about reducing exposure to that trigger.

F is incorrect because it is too strong of a statement when it says, "there would be no way…" By taking extreme measures, for instance, it would be possible to prevent exposure to a trigger, even if that trigger was unknown. G is incorrect because it would be, in theory, possible to test for every trigger imaginable. H is, at first glance, appealing. It is, however, incorrect because it refers to the specific phrasing used in lines 13-14, which state, "It not yet certain if there is a single, greater underlying cause for asthma," and the underlying cause for asthma has nothing to do with combatting asthma by taking preventive measures. K may also seem appealing initially, but is incorrect because "obvious" does not mean "visible to the human eye."

MATH EXPLANATIONS ▶

Answer Explanations – Mathematics
Practice Test 1

51. **(E)** To solve this, you must first remember that an operation involving the division of a fraction must be treated as a multiplication of the reciprocal of the fraction.

$$5.6 \div \frac{7}{4} = 5.6 \times \frac{4}{7} =$$

$$\frac{\overset{8}{\cancel{56}}}{\cancel{10}_{5}} \times \frac{\cancel{4}^{2}}{\cancel{7}_{1}} = \frac{16}{5} =$$

$$3\frac{1}{5} = 3.2$$

52. **(K)** Betty needs an average of 92 across 6 tests. Her total score for the 6 tests has to be

$92 \times 6 = 552$.

Next, find the sum of Betty's first 5 tests.

$88 + 91 + 99 + 86 + 92 = 456$.

Subtract 456 from 552 to find the answer:

$552 - 456 = 96$

That's how much Betty needs to at least score.

53. **(D)** To solve this, first subtract 5 from 14 to get 9. That is how old Jaime was then.

Next, realize that 9 was one-third of his uncle's age then. This means that his uncle was 27 then.

To find Jaime's uncle's current age, add 5 to 27, which is 32.

54. **(F)** To solve this problem, rearrange the equation to get y by itself on one side.

From, $14x - 7y - 4 = 45$, add $7y$ to both sides. This gives:

$14x - 4 = 7y + 45$

Then subtract 45 from both sides. This gives:

$14x - 49 = 7y$

Finally, divide both sides of the equation by 7 to get:

$2x - 7 = y$

55. **(C)** First, set up an equation:

$4x + 2 \times 7 = 62$,

where 2×7 represents the combined length of the 2 red curtains and x represents the length of one purple curtain. Then solve for x:

$4x = 62 - 14 = 48$

Dividing by 4 on each side, we get:

$x = 12$

56. **(G)** Rounding 3.1647 to the nearest hundredth gives 3.16.

The question is, in essence, asking for the difference between 3.1672 and 3.16. This means:

$3.1672 - 3.16 = 0.0072$

57. **(A)** Remember that prime factors are factors that are also prime numbers. Also remember that 1 is not prime, while 2 is. The quickest way to solve this problem is to eliminate answer choices that contain factors that are not prime. 10 and 6 are also not prime. Thus, B, C, D, and E can be safely and quickly eliminated.

---

58. **(K)** Because the answers are expressed in fractions, it is easier to convert all of the percentages to fractions first.

$$S = \frac{1}{4}T$$

$$T = \frac{2}{{}_4\cancel{100}} \times \cancel{25}^{\,1} = \frac{2}{4} = \frac{1}{2}$$

Substituting T into the first equation, we get:

$$S = \frac{1}{4}\left(\frac{1}{2}\right) = \frac{1}{8}$$

---

59. **(B)** Distributing $4xy$ across all of the terms inside the parentheses gives:

$20xywz - 12xyu$

---

60. **(J)** If $A - B$ is even, that means that A and B are either both even or both odd, but not one of each. The same is true of B and C. And because B stays the same, A and C are either both odd or both even.

Thus, J is the solution because no matter whether A and C are even or odd, their sum will be even, which makes H incorrect. F is incorrect because if A and C are even, then $A \times C$ is even. The opposite is true of G, which makes it incorrect. K is incorrect because A may be smaller than C.

61. **(C)** To solve this problem, first convert all of the percentages to decimal numbers:

$700\% = 7$, and $7\% = .07$

Next, do the required multiplications, remembering that the word "of" in mathematics refers to multiplication:

$7 \times 7 = 49$;

$.07 \times 70 = 4.9$

Next, perform the required subtraction:

$49 - 4.9 = 44.1$

---

62. **(H)** The best way to approach this problem is to pick a value of n that would give the expression of $n + 7$ a remainder of 4 when divided by 5.

One such value of n is 7.

$7 + 7 = 14$, which gives a remainder of 4 when divided by 5.

Dividing 7 by 5, we see that the remainder is 2. Try this with other viable values of n, and you will get the same result.

---

63. **(C)** If the side of the square is 9 cm, then the radius of the circle is 4.5 cm, since the diameter of the circle has the same length as that of a side of the square.

The area of a circle is expressed by: $A = \pi r^2$. Substituting 4.5 in for r, we get:

$A = \pi(4.5)^2 = 20.25\pi \text{ cm}^2$

---

64. **(F)** Substituting 6.25 in for w and 3.75 in for z, we get:

$(6.25 + 3.75)(6.25 - 3.75) = (10)(2.5) = 25$

65. **(D)** Solve for m by first multiplying each side by 7: $2(m - 6) = 42$

Then divide each side by 2:

$m - 6 = 21$

Add 6 to each side to get $m = 27$

66. **(J)** Citysville's population in 1990 was roughly 200,000. 300% of 200,000 is 600,000. This means that Citysville's population was approximately 300% of its 1990 population in 1996.

67. **(E)** First, multiply both sides of the equation by 4:

$4z = 4(2w + 3) = 8w + 12$

The subtract 5 from each side.

$4z - 5 = 8w + 12 - 5 = 8w + 7$

68. **(G)** $4n - 5$ represents the total number of fliers that Ashley and Bobby handed out. In other words:

$A + B = 4n - 5$

We know that Bobby's total is 5 more than Ashley's:

$B = A + 5$

Substituting $A + 5$ in for B in the first equation, we get the following:

$A + (A + 5) = 4n - 5$

$2A + 5 = 4n - 5$ → $2A = 4n - 10$

To find Ashley's total, divide each side by 2:

$A = 2n - 5$

69. **(A)** Dividing A8,C49,FGH.KLM by 10,000 gives A,8C4.9FGHKLM. The thousandths place is therefore G.

70. **(K)** First, convert 480 minutes to hours. Dividing by 60, we find that the cellist practiced 8 hours on the second day.

Her practice total in 3 days is 24 hours. She thus needs to practice 11 more hours in the remainder of the week. The next step is to convert 11 hours into seconds:

11 hr × 3,600 sec/hr = 39,600 seconds.

71. **(D)** First, multiply the both the numerator and denominator by 10 to get rid of the decimal place. Next, simplify the expression by dividing by 4, which is the largest common factor:

$$\frac{68}{16K} \rightarrow \frac{17}{4K}$$

For the expression to be the smallest positive integer, the expression should have a value of 1. Solving for K, we multiply both sides by K.

$$\frac{17}{4K} = 1 \rightarrow \frac{17}{4} = K$$

72. **(J)** According to the problem, m is positive and n is negative. Solve this problem by eliminating incorrect possibilities.

F is incorrect because n^2 is positive, and may be greater m. G is incorrect because if m2 is greater than n, then the sum will be positive. H is incorrect because n^2, a positive value, may be larger than m^2. K is incorrect because $m^2 + n^2$ must be positive.

73. **(E)** The best way to approach this problem is to divide the hexagon into a rectangle and two identical triangles to each side of the rectangle, by drawing two lines straight down from the top two vertices to the bottom two vertices.

Count to see that the length of the rectangle is 11 cm and that the width of the rectangle is 6 cm. The triangles have a base of 11 cm, since their bases share a side with the rectangle. The triangles have a height of 3 cm.

To summarize, the dimensions of the rectangle and triangles are as follows:

- Rectangle: 11 cm by 6 cm
- Each triangle: 3 cm by 11 cm

In order to find the area of land needed, in terms of square feet, each side length must be converted to feet:

- Rect.: 44 yd by 24 yd = 132 ft by 72 ft
- Tri.: 12 yd by 44 yd = 36 ft by 132 ft

The total area is, then, as follows:

Rectangle's area + 2 × Triangle's area =

$(132 \times 72) + 2 \times \frac{1}{2}(36 \times 132) =$

9,504 sq ft + 4,752 sq ft = 14,256 sq ft

74. **(G)** The jar originally contained 24 beads. After the three beads are removed, there are 21 beads. Of the 21 beads, 7 are orange, since two were removed. This means that Kelly's probability of drawing a bead that isn't orange is:

$$1 - \frac{7}{21} = \frac{14}{21} = \frac{2}{3}$$

75. **(E)** Subtract 8 from m and set that equal to one-fourth of George's age then:

$$m - 8 = \frac{1}{4}(g - 8)$$

Solving for m, we get:

$$m = \frac{1}{4}g - 2 + 8 = \frac{1}{4}g + 6$$

g has to be a multiple of 4. Notice, though, that g must be greater than 8. Otherwise, m would be less than or equal to 0. Thus, the smallest value of g is 12, and $m = 9$. Of course, g could theoretically be 16, 20, etc., but the largest value of m listed as an answer choice is 9.

76. **(J)** The width of the garden can be found by multiplying ¾ and 24:

$w = ¾ \times 24 = 18$ feet

Next, we must convert the dimensions to yards, which require us to divide each side by 3. Then, when we multiply the results, we get:

$l \times w = 8$ yd × 6 yd = 48 sq yd

77. **(C)** It is important to realize that the two angles depicted in the figure are supplementary and thus add to 180°: $x + y = 180$

Furthermore, $y = 1.5x$. After substitution:

$x + 1.5x = 2.5x = 180$

Dividing each side by 2.5 to get $x = 72$. This means that $y = 108$.

Plugging the values of x and y into $2y - x$, we get:

$2(108) - 72 = 144$

78. **(H)** To solve this, write an equation for the perimeter of the polygon, as follows:

$$4m + 3(m + 2) + 3(2m - 3) + 9 + 11 + 15 = 97$$

Next, rewrite this as:

$$4m + (3m + 6) + (6m - 9) + 9 + 11 + 15 = 97$$

Add like terms to get $13m + 32 = 97$

After subtracting 32 from each side, we get

$13m = 65$, so $m = 5$, after dividing each side by 13.

79. **(A)** By evaluating x and y, we get:

$$x = 6 + 8 = 14, \text{ and } y = \sqrt{100} = 10$$

Thus, $x - y = 14 - 10 = 4$

80. **(G)** If one centimeter on a map represents 100 miles, 1 square centimeter represents 10,000 square miles.

Divide 10,000 by 1,000 to get 10 square miles. Dividing 1 square centimeter by 1,000, we see that 0.001 sq cm represents 10 square miles.

81. **(D)** By subtracting the coordinate values of O from R and O from P, we get the lengths of OP and OR, respectively:

$$OR = 11 - (^-5) = 11 + 5 = 16, \text{ and}$$

$$OP = {}^-1 - (^-5) = {}^-1 + 5 = 4$$

To find the difference of the lengths of the segments, all you have to do is subtract OR from OP to get 12.

82. **(H)** First, we must divide 469 by 15 and find the remainder.

$$469 \div 15 = 31 \text{ R4}$$

Thus, H is the correct answer. The part about the bench seating for 540 is extraneous information and can be ignored.

83. **(B)** Arranging the number of park patrons in order from least to greatest, we get:

98, 153, 153, 177, 186, 194, 203, 203

Because there is an even number of number of patron numbers, to find the median, we must take the average of the middle two numbers.

$$(177 + 186) \div 2 = 181.5$$

84. **(K)** To solve this problem, find the fraction of worker bees collected to the total number of bees collected. Then multiply this fraction by 4,500 to get the estimate of worker bees in the apiary:

$$\frac{35}{75} = \frac{7}{15} \text{ is the ratio of workers to the total.}$$

$$\frac{7}{15} \times 4,500 = 2,100 \text{ worker bees}$$

85. **(D)** To find the area of the shaded region, first find the area of half of the square. Then, subtract half of the area of the circle (which has a radius of 3) shown in the diagram from the half of the area of the square:

Area of ½-square: $\frac{1}{2} \times 14 \times 14 = 98$

Area of ½-circle: $\frac{1}{2} \times \pi \times 3^2 = 4.5\pi$

After subtraction, we get: $98 - 4.5\pi$

86. **(H)** If 660 feet = 1 furlong, and there are 8 furlongs in a mile, then that means there are 5,280 feet in a mile. This means that there are 15,840 feet in one league. In 2.5 leagues, there are 39,600 feet. There are 13,200 yards, then.

---

87. **(A)** Jimmy ran 15 laps, based on the calculation of

$$\frac{5}{\cancel{13}_{1}} \times \cancel{39}^{3} = 15$$

If each lap is a quarter mile, we must divide 15 by 4 to find the number of miles Jimmy ran. The answer is thus 3.75 miles.

---

88. **(K)** If Ash is a years old, and Cal is 5 years younger than Ash, Cal is $a - 5$ years old. In 14 years, Cal will be:

$$(a - 5) + 14 = a + 9 \text{ years old}$$

---

89. **(A)** Between Rob and Ty, the two ate:

$$\frac{5}{12} + 3\left(\frac{5}{12}\right) = \frac{20}{12} \text{ or } 1\frac{8}{12} = 1\frac{2}{3} \text{ of a pie.}$$

That means the amount of pie that's left uneaten is

$$3 - 1\frac{2}{3} = 1\frac{1}{3} \text{ or } \frac{4}{3}$$

The ratio of the amount of pie eaten to uneaten is

$$\frac{5}{3} : \frac{4}{3} \text{ or } 5 : 3$$

90. **(J)** The losing student collected 40% of the 3,500 votes, which means he received 1,400 votes.

The problem is asking for the percentage of the total student body:

$$\frac{1,400}{4,000} \times 100\% = 35\%$$

---

91. **(A)** Solve for q by first multiplying each side by 8:

$$5p - 2q = 32q$$

Then add $2q$ to each side:

$$5p = 34q$$

Divide each side by 34:

$$\frac{5p}{34} = q$$

---

92. **(H)** From 1 to 202, there are 67 multiples of 3. The 67th multiple of 3 is 201.

There are 33 multiples of 6 within that same range of numbers, with the 33rd multiple of 6 being 198.

Thus, the correct answer is $67 - 33 = 34$.

---

93. **(C)** If Lee ate 6 green jelly beans from a bag, he'll have 46 jelly beans left over, with 6 of them being green:

Total: $52 - 6 = 46$; Green: $12 - 6 = 6$

The probability that the next jelly bean he picks will be green is:

$$\frac{6}{46} = \frac{3}{23}$$

94. (J) It takes the arrow 10 seconds to make one complete revolution, since it rotates at 6 revolutions per 1 minute or 60 seconds. To get to F for the fifteenth time, the arrow will have to have spun 14 complete revolutions (140 seconds), and then during the course of the 15th revolution, it will land on F for the 15th time.

Furthermore, it takes the arrow one-eighth of 10 seconds (for a total of 1.25 seconds) to go from wedge to wedge, i.e., from A to C or E to G. There are 5 such wedges that the arrow has to travel across to get from A to F, meaning that it takes the arrow 6.25 seconds to get from A to F.

Thus, the total time it will take the arrow to point to F for the 15th time is 140 + 6.25, or 146.25, seconds.

---

95. (B) Set up an equation for the perimeter of the parallelogram, such as:

$106 = 2s + 2l$, where s represents the value of AB and CD, and l represents the value of BC and AD.

We know that BC and AD are 48:

$106 = 2s + 96$

Rearranging the equation to find for s:

$2s = 106 - 96 = 10 \rightarrow s = 5$

Then, to find the area of triangle ABE, we first need to apply the Pythagorean Theorem to find BE:

$5^2 = 4^2 + (BE)^2 \rightarrow (BE)^2 = 25 - 16 = 9$

Solving for BE, we get BE = 3.

And then by applying the formula to find the area of a triangle, we get:

Area = ½ × 4 (base) × 3 (height) = 6 sq cm

96. (F) If the dimensions are reduced by 50%, the sides become 7.5 feet, 9 inches, and 3 feet. Convert to yards to get:

Length: 7.5 feet = 2.5 yards
Width: 9 in = 0.25 yards
Height: 3 ft = 1 yard

The volume of the block is: 2.5 × 0.25 × 1 = 0.625 cubic yards

---

97. (B) ABCD, shown below, represents the steel cage with dimensions of 40 feet by 90 feet. The tiger is tied to a corner of the cage by a rope that's $40\sqrt{2}$ feet long, which is the diagonal of the square AEFD. DG is also $40\sqrt{2}$ feet, but it exists outside of square AEFD, and the tiger can travel from E to G in a circular arc.

The total area the tiger can roam is the sum of the area of triangle ADE and the area of sector DEG, which is one-eighth of the area of circle D (with segments DE and DG comprising two radii), since angle EDG measures 45°. (Remember segment DE makes up the diagonal of square AEFD.)

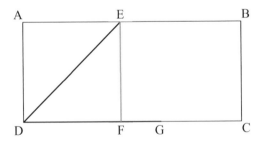

Area of triangle ADE = ½ × 40 × 40 = 800

Area of sector DEG = $\dfrac{45°}{360°} \times \pi \times \left(40\sqrt{2}\right)^2$

$$= \dfrac{1}{8} \times \pi \times 3,200 = 400\pi$$

The total area that the tiger can roam is therefore 400(2 + π) square feet.

98. (J) If two opposite corners of a square have coordinates of (0, 0) and (0, 5), this means that the diagonal of the square is 5 units in length.

If the diagonal of a square is 5 units long, then the sides of the square have lengths of $5\sqrt{2}$ units. (This can be ascertained by using the Pythagorean Theorem, worked out below.) By squaring the side length (or s^2, in other words), we can find the area.

Below is a partially worked out Pythagorean Theorem, without actually finding s, since s^2 is all we need to find:

$5^2 = 2s^2$, where s represents the side length.

$25 = 2s^2 \rightarrow s^2 = 12.5$

---

99. (A) This problem is one of simplification.

$$\frac{1}{4}\left[8\left(\frac{1-2}{2+3}\right)\left(\frac{3+2}{2-1}\right)\right] =$$

$$\frac{1}{\cancel{4}_1}\left[\cancel{8}^2\left(\frac{1-2}{\cancel{2+3}_1}\right)\left(\frac{\cancel{3+2}^1}{2-1}\right)\right]$$

It should be noted that $(2-1) = {}^{-}(1-2)$. Thus, when these terms are divided, they simplify to $^{-}1$.

So when everything is simplified, we get $^{-}2$ as the answer.

100. (K) This problem requires a series of steps.

$MQ = MN + NQ = 20$ cm

$MN + NQ = 20 \rightarrow MN + 15 = 20$

$MN = 5$

Furthermore,

$MP = MN + NP = 8$ cm

$8 = 5 + NP \rightarrow NP = 3$ cm

From this, we can find that PQ from:

$NQ = NP + PQ$.

$15 = 3 + PQ \rightarrow PQ = 12$

This also gives us:

$NP = NO + OP = 3$ cm $\rightarrow$ OP = 2 cm, since OP = 2(NO).

To solve for OQ, we must do:

$OQ = OP + PQ$

$OQ = 2 + 12 = 14$ cm

SHSAT
TJHSST EDITION
TEST KEY 2

Answer Key – Test 2

VERBAL

SCRAMBLED PARAGRAPHS

Paragraph 1
RQTUS

Paragraph 2
URSQT

Paragraph 3
RUTSQ

Paragraph 4
TURSQ

Paragraph 5
RTQSU

LOGICAL REASONING

11. D
12. K
13. E
14. J
15. D
16. G
17. A
18. F
19. E
20. H
21. B
22. K
23. D
24. F
25. D

READING

26. G
27. D
28. J
29. C
30. F
31. B
32. G
33. D
34. K
35. A
36. H
37. E
38. J
39. B
40. J
41. C
42. G
43. E
44. F
45. E
46. H
47. D
48. K
49. C
50. G

MATH ANSWERS ▶

Answer Key – Test 2

MATHEMATICS

51.	E	**76.**	G
52.	J	**77.**	E
53.	B	**78.**	J
54.	H	**79.**	D
55.	C	**80.**	K
56.	G	**81.**	C
57.	A	**82.**	G
58.	J	**83.**	C
59.	A	**84.**	G
60.	G	**85.**	B
61.	A	**86.**	F
62.	J	**87.**	E
63.	E	**88.**	J
64.	J	**89.**	D
65.	C	**90.**	J
66.	G	**91.**	E
67.	D	**92.**	F
68.	K	**93.**	A
69.	C	**94.**	H
70.	G	**95.**	A
71.	E	**96.**	H
72.	G	**97.**	E
73.	B	**98.**	G
74.	H	**99.**	B
75.	A	**100.**	J

VERBAL EXPLANATIONS ▶

AE

Answer Explanations – Verbal
Practice Test 2

SCRAMBLED PARAGRAPHS

Paragraph 1 (RQTUS)

The lead sentence introduces iron as Earth's most abundant elements. And because it is so abundant, iron would not be considered a precious metal by most people.

Sentence R follows the lead because it elaborates on the lead sentence and provides perspective about iron's value. Q follows R because it establishes a contrast to R and introduces the idea that iron has is important because of its usefulness.

After Q, it is possible to cluster T, U, and S, in that order. T discusses the first time iron's usefulness was discovered by the Hittites. U follows up with more information on the Hittites and the fall of their empire, which ushered in the Iron Age. S serves as the conclusion.

Note: It may be tempting to select S after Q, but the problem is the phrase "ever since then" in S. If S followed directly after Q, there would be no "then" to for the beginning of S to refer to.

Paragraph 2 (URSQT)

The opening sentence states that the Soviet Union made history by being the first country to launch an artificial satellite that could and did orbit Earth. Sentence U follows the lead because it provides the name of the satellite. R follows U because it introduces how Sputnik's impact was large, namely in that the American public's confidence was shaken.

S follows R with its mention of how the American public's confidence was not helped by the knowledge that the Soviet Union had used intercontinental ballistic missiles to launch Sputnik I. Q comes after S because Q further elaborates on why

it was a big deal that the Soviet Union used a modified ballistic missile to launch Sputnik. T comes last because it serves as the conclusion by telling how the United States responded to assuage the fears of Americans and by shifting focus to another possible discussion point.

Note: It may be tempting to select sentence T after selecting R because R discusses the deterioration of the American public's confidence and T discusses what the United States did to try to remedy the anxiety and tension the Americans felt. The problem with placing T immediately after R is that the latter portion of T makes for an awkward transition to the other sentences that would follow.

Paragraph 3 (RUTSQ)

The opening sentence makes it apparent that the passage will be about papyrus, paper, or both. Sentence R comes after the lead because it tells how papyrus was different from paper. Specifically, it tells that papyrus was more of a mat made of interwoven papyrus reeds or stalks. U comes after R because it tells what happens before papyrus reeds were interwoven into a mat. T comes after U because it tells why the reeds of papyrus were soaked in water to allow rotting.

S follows T because it provides the transition from the discussion of papyrus to the invention of modern day paper. Q follows S because it acknowledges that T'sai Lun may not have been the true inventor of paper but that he is generally credited as paper's inventor because he was the first one to have recorded the paper-making process.

Easy Clusters: RUT and SQ are the easiest clusters to make. From there, it should be obvious that SQ cannot precede RUT, which means that the correct order is RUTSQ.

Paragraph 4 (TURSQ)

The lead sentence makes it clear that skin color plays a biological role, although it is not apparent from the first sentence what that role is.

T comes after the lead because it introduces how skin color may make a difference by stating that lighter skin typically produces more vitamin D_3 than darker skin does. U comes after T because the pronouns "it" and "its" in U is referring to the lighter skin mentioned in T. Otherwise, U wouldn't make sense because U is still comparing lighter skin and darker skin.

R comes after U because R expounds upon melanin, which is introduced by U. R also states that melanin helps reduce photodamage by absorbing and scattering UVB radiation. S follows R because it discusses the tradeoff to being able to absorb more UVB radiation.

Finally, Q comes last because it wraps the paragraph up by issuing warnings for both lighter and darker skinned people. *Hint:* The word ultimately should have tipped you off to some degree that Q was the concluding sentence.

Tip: If you had difficulty in selecting the first sentence after the lead, then focus first on connecting the dots between the sentences. You'll soon see that TURS are all linked together, which leaves either T or Q to be the sentence after the lead. It makes a lot more sense for T to come right after the lead and not Q, and once you make that connection, the correct order becomes apparent.

Paragraph 5 (RTQSU)

The introductory sentence of the paragraph introduces the pirate Blackbeard as one of the most feared pirates from 1716 to 1718.

Sentence R comes after the introductory sentence because it is the only sentence to introduce Blackbeard by what is believed to be his full name; no other sentence refers to Blackbeard as Edward Teach. It also states that Teach served under Captain Benjamin Hornigold. T follows R because it

continues the discussion of Teach's time with Hornigold. Q comes after T because it continues with the discussion of his new ship, which was introduced as *Queen Anne's Revenge* in T.

S describes why the colonists put up with Blackbeard even though he terrorized the American and Caribbean coasts. U comes after S and concludes the paragraph, as it follows on S's statement that Teach's criminal reign didn't last a long time.

Tip: If it was difficult to immediately connect S and Q, think about making clusters with RTQ and SU. Then either S comes after Q or R comes after U. It makes much more sense for S to come after Q than for R to come after U. Thus, the correct order is RTQSU.

Logical Reasoning

11. **(D)** There are two ways to solve this problem. The first is to draw a chart or table.

	1	2	3	4	5	6	7
H	X	X	X	X	X		
S	X	X	X		X		
M	X	X	X	X			
E					X	X	

The second, and perhaps more reliable, method is to find the total number of times he'll study all of the subjects. Since he will study history 5 times, science and math 4 times each, and English 2 times, he will have studied for a total of 15 subjects in the upcoming week.

With a maximum of 3 different subjects per day, the theoretical most number of days he studies three subjects in a given day is $15 \div 3$, which leads to 5. And, as we can see from the chart above, this is indeed possible, and therefore the correct answer.

Note: Using the chart method can be misleading. It is easy to get 4 as the correct answer, but we have just shown that it is not the case.

12. **(K)** The only possible logical conclusion that can be made here is that all Hentown farmers are over two meters tall. In Hentown, only adults can be farmers, based on the second sentence of the problem, and all adults in Hentown are over two meters tall. This means that all farmers in Hentown are over two meters tall.

F is incorrect because it contradicts the last statement of the problem, that some farmers are athletes. G is incorrect because the last sentence of the problem does not specify that some Hentown farmers are athletes. It is possible to conclude that none of the Hentown farmers are athletes. H is incorrect. As it was pointed out before, it is erroneous to conclude that any Hentown farmer is also a athlete. Furthermore, even if it were true that some

Hentown farmers are athletes, that would not necessarily mean every athlete in Hentown is a farmer. J is incorrect because the problem doesn't discuss Hentown children, so we cannot draw conclusions about them.

13. **(E)** Bobby is the fastest kid in his class, and he can run a mile in 6 minutes. That does not, however, mean Teresa is in his class. If so, that would mean she could be faster than he is. It is also possible that Teresa is in Bobby's class but still won the race, if Bobby did not participate in the race or if he did not run as fast as he could, for whatever reason. There are very many unknowns here, and E is the only choice that addresses these possibilities.

A is incorrect because it contradicts the first sentence of the problem. B is incorrect because it is possible Teresa is in Bobby's class and still won the race. C is incorrect because there is not information to support it—it is impossible to tell from this problem how fast Teresa can run. D is incorrect because it is possible that Bobby entered the race and lost.

14. **(J)** Draw a diagram of the different square formations of people that can be made.

As you can see, when people make up the squares, it isn't a simple matter of $4 \times (3 + 4 + 5) = 48$, which is probably the most tempting answer choice. It isn't the same as taking the perimeter of each square because the 4 corners of each square can't be counted twice, which is what would happen if only the perimeter were being found. Thus, for each square, the total number of people is $p - 4$, where p represents the perimeter value. This means that for 3 squares, the total number of people used is the sum of the perimeters minus 12.

It is also possible to count the dots to arrive at the correct answer: $8 + 12 + 16 = 36$.

15. **(D)** This question tests the use of logic statements. There are two conditional statements in this problem.

The first statement reads, "Moe will not attend the fair if Jay does." Note that the hypothesis and conclusion of this statement are switched in order of presentation. In other words, it can be rewritten as "If Jay attends the fair, Moe will not attend." The contrapositive of this statement, then, is "If Moe attends the fair, Jay did/will not."

The second statement reads "Jay will attend the fair if Ann is able to get to Jay's house on time." Again, this conditional statement is written in reverse order. Rearranging it, it becomes "If Ann is able to get to Jay's house on time, Jay will attend the fair." The contrapositive of this statement is "If Jay does not attend the fair, Ann wasn't able to get to Jay's house on time."

A is wrong because it is not certain what Moe will do if Jay does not attend the fair. We only know that if Jay does, then Moe will not, and that If Moe does, then Jay will or did not. B is wrong because it is possible that either Moe or Jay will attend the fair. C and D are incorrect because the link between Moe and Ann's attendance has not been established in the problem. This leaves D as the only viable choice.

D works. If Ann is able to get to Jay's house on time, then Jay will attend the fair. And if Jay attends the fair, then Moe will not. This sort of logical deduction adheres to and is governed by what is known as the law of syllogism.

16. **(G)** The best way to approach this problem is to draw a chart or diagram that ranks the girls' bubble-blowing prowess.

Based on the statements, the only position we can fill in is Zelma's. We know that May's bubble popped right before Tara's did. That means that May's bubble is immediately smaller than Tara's. From this, we can deduce, then, that Wanda's bubble was also immediately smaller than Val's bubble because there would be only two slots left, if we filled in Tara and May into a chart diagram.

Thus, having established that Wanda and Val are positioned immediately next to each other, there are only two possible rankings of the girls' bubble sizes:

Biggest Bubble

1.	Tara	Val
2.	May	Wanda
3.	Zelma	
4.	Val	Tara
5.	Wanda	May

Smallest Bubble

F is wrong because it is impossible for Val to have blown the smallest bubble. H is wrong because it is not possible for Wanda to have blown the biggest bubble. J is incorrect because May could not have blown the second smallest bubble. It is important to pay attention to the wording of the answer choices, if J is the choice you selected; it does not say May blew the second biggest bubble. K is incorrect because Tara's bubble had to have popped either last or right after Zelma's.

This leaves G as the only working choice, and it is correct. If you concluded G was wrong, make sure to reread the wording carefully.

17. **(A)** Draw a diagram or chart to solve this problem and fill in as much information as possible.

First in Line

1.		
2.	Sasha	
3.	Pat	
4.	Trey	Pat
5.		Trey

Last in Line

From the clues presented, the above diagram shows the only possibilities. Thus, we know that Pay is either 3rd or 4th and Trey is either 4th or 5th in line, since Trey is right behind Pat in line. A is correct. If Ursula is third, then Roger has to be first, and the precise order of the line can be solved.

B is incorrect because Pat cannot be first in line. C is wrong because Roger *may* be first in line, but it is not necessarily true that he is. D is wrong because if Roger is 3rd, then Ursula must be 1st. E is incorrect because Sasha *may* be two places ahead of Trey but not necessarily so.

18. **(F)** This problem involves, at its core, a series of conditional statements, which can be rewritten as:

   1) $S \rightarrow \sim M$
   2) $S \rightarrow \sim B$
   3) $O \rightarrow \sim S$
   4) $B \rightarrow \sim M$

Note: ~ means "not." As such, the first conditional statement should be read, "If S, then not M." Of course that in itself is an abbreviated form of "If Aimee goes to the sports event, she will not go to the museum."

For simplicity, the first conditional statement was broken down into two. By looking at these conditional statements, it is possible to figure out the contrapositives.

   1) $M \rightarrow \sim S$
   2) $B \rightarrow \sim S$
   3) $S \rightarrow \sim O$
   4) $M \rightarrow \sim B$

From the above, it is possible to conclude that if Aimee goes to two cultural events in a week, she could not have gone to the sports event, since she cannot go to the opera house if she goes to the sports event. If she wants to go to the sports event, then that can be the only event she goes to in that week, which rules out H.

If Aimee goes to the museum, she cannot go to the sports event or the book club. This leaves the opera house. And if Amy goes to the book club, she cannot go to the museum or sports event. This again leaves the opera house. Thus, if Amy were to attend two cultural events, one of them must be the opera house. The other one can be either the museum or book club, but not both, thus ruling out G and J. K is ruled out because Amy *is* able to attend two cultural events per week, based on the facts.

19. **(E)** Draw a diagram or chart, keeping in mind that you have to keep track of books and colors.

Based on the first three numbered facts, two possible arrangements of the books seem to arise. They are as follows:

First possibility:

L				R
1	2	3	4	5
E	M	P		
R	B			Y

Second possibility:

L				R
1	2	3	4	5
E		M	P	
R			B	Y

The above possibilities show the econ book as leftmost and the math and psychology books as adjacent, with math to the immediate left of the psychology book.

Once we throw in the fourth numbered clue, however, it becomes clear that the second possibility does not work because the blue book has to be to the left of the green book, but there is no space to the blue book's right. Thus, the first possibility is the correct one and requires the green book to come between the blue and yellow books. This leaves the orange book as the leftmost on the shelf.

20. **(H)** Use the process of elimination to answer this question.

F is incorrect. Strictly based on the passage, India's population could be more than 1.3 billion. G is incorrect; no reference point to the Pitcairn Islands is given. While it is possible that the Cocos Islands is the least populous nation, it may not be. The only thing we know is that the Cocos Islands has a smaller population than the Pitcairn Islands does. J is incorrect; again, no reference point is established as to the Pitcairn Islands. K is incorrect; the problem doesn't provide enough information to compare the populations of China and India.

H is correct. India's population is second greatest. Vietnam has a bigger population than Thailand does. This means Vietnam is, in the absence of information, at best third most populous. And if Vietnam is third most populous, then Thailand is at best fourth most populous.

21. **(B)** To solve this problem, the best way is to draw out a chart or diagram.

There are exactly four possibilities because Rena passes the carum immediately before she passes the violet. Based on this information only, the following diagram can be constructed:

First Flower Passed

1.	D			
2.	C			
3.	V	C		
4.		V	C	
5.			V	C
6.				V

Last Flower Passed

And because the problem indicates that Rena passes the tulip before she passes the lily, which she passes before the rose, the chart can be filled in as shown below:

First Flower Passed

1.	D	D	D	D
2.	C	T	T	T
3.	V	C	L	L
4.	T	V	C	R
5.	L	L	V	C
6.	R	R	R	V

Last Flower Passed

Based on this chart, we can eliminate every choice but B. In every case, the lily is either third or fifth.

22. **(K)** This question is best solved by drawing a table or diagram.

First Animal Presented

1.	
2.	Nightingale
3.	
4.	Finny – Aardvark
5.	Iguana

Last Animal Presented

Because the crocodile and swordfish were both presented before the aardvark was, the aardvark was presented fourth by Finny.

From the facts, it is not possible to say whether the crocodile or swordfish was presented first; nor is it possible to that either was presented third. This rules out both F and G. H is incorrect because Dolores could not have presented the iguana, since she presented before Georgette did. J is not possible either because Georgette could not have presented last, since Finny presented fourth, and according to the facts, Dolores presented immediately before Georgette did.

23. **(D)** If the smallest member of the Tiger scores four goals every game, then it is not possible that Bret is the smallest member of the Tigers, if he scored five goals, thus effectively ruling out choice A. It also makes D a valid statement.

B is unsupported by the facts. Just because the smallest player on the team scores the most goals per game, on average, does not mean that smaller players average more goals per game. C is incorrect because it is possible for a player on the Tigers to score more than the smallest member in a game. E is incorrect because it is not supported by the facts at all.

24. **(F)** For "decoding sentence" question types, try to figure out what as many of the letters mean as possible.

    Here, every sentence contains the word "and". Since every coded sentence also contains the letter P, it is possible to conclude that the letter P stands for the word "and." Because the question is asking which letter represents "Louis," it is important to decode as many of the words in the third sentence as possible. By looking at the first and third sentences, it is possible to determine that L stands for "water." The second and third sentences reveal that J stands for "pizza." Finally, the third and fourth sentences show that A represents "likes." Because the letters P, A, L, and J have been decoded, R is left as the only choice in the third sentence and thus represents "Louis."

25. **(D)** The only time "eats" appears is in the second sentence. Incidentally, "Clara" also only appears in the second sentence, indicating that there may be some uncertainty as to which letter represents which word. The word "lasagna" also appears in the fourth sentence, and we can conclude that Y stands for "lasagna," having already established J as "pizza" and P as "and."

    This leaves K or T to represent either "Clara" or "eats." At this point, answer choice E may seem the most alluring, but that is not the correct answer. The reason for this is that the rules listed above questions 24 and 25 state that "the position of a letter is never the same as that of the word it represents." The letter K cannot, therefore, represent "Clara" and instead represents "eats." D is the correct answer choice.

READING ▶

AE

READING

(Ironclads)

26. **(G)** This passage is mainly about the Civil War ironclads *Virginia* and *Monitor*, how they met, how they fought, and the significance of their role in the Battle of Hampton Roads. Thus, G is the best answer. The other answer choices of F, H, and J, while certainly mentioned in the passage, do not fully encompass why the passage was written. K is incorrect because the passage does not suggest that the Confederacy lost the Civil War because *Virginia* could not defeat *Monitor*.

27. **(D)** Lines 11-21 indicate that *Virginia* had been deployed in order to break through the blockade that the Union had set up, so D is correct.

    A is incorrect. While it is certainly suggested that *Virginia* was significantly more powerful than non-ironclad ships (lines 7-9), the passage does not imply that ironclads were invincible to damage by wooden ships. B is incorrect because it, too, is an overreaching statement. Certainly, the Confederacy was trying to break through the Union's blockade because it was restricting the Confederacy's ability to trade freely. But that does not mean that Virginia was the only Confederate state that could trade internationally. And, perhaps it would not be an invalid conclusion to draw that Virginia was the only Confederate state that could trade internationally, based solely on the passage, but it would also not be an invalid conclusion to draw that Virginia was not the only one. C is unsupported. E is also unsupported. Granted, it may have appeared that the two ironclads were locked in stalemate, with neither side being able to unequivocally vanquish the other, but it would logically fallacious to assume that it was impossible for a clear victor to have eventually emerged.

28. **(J)** The best way to answer this question is to figure out which questions in the answer choices are answered by the passage. F is answered in lines 23-24. *Monitor* came to aid the defense of the grounded *Minnesota*. G is answered in lines 9-11. CSS *Virginia* had previously served as USS *Merrimack*. H is answered in lines 29-30. One of the commanding officers of *Monitor* was Lieutenant John L. Worden. K is answered in lines 7-8. Virginia had defeated *Congress* and *Cumberland* on March 8, 1862, since the passage reads, "On March 9, 1862, a day after handily defeating USS *Congress* and *Cumberland* […]" Thus, the only remaining choice is J, which is correct.

29. **(C)** The best way to answer this question is to eliminate incorrect answers. A is incorrect because it is an overreaching statement in that it says wooden warships were terminated *immediately* after the Civil War was over. The problem lies in the word "immediately." The passage does state, in lines 47-48, that the era of wooden naval vessels was nigh, but it does not state or suggest that the vessels were decommissioned immediately after the Civil War. B is incorrect because it is not known at all whether *Virginia*'s smokestack was reinforced with heavy armor plating. Just because the smokestack was blown off does not mean that it was not reinforced with heavy armor plating. D is incorrect because it is not known whether *Monitor* could have won, even if it had not been defending *Minnesota*. E is also not supported by the passage. There is nothing to indicate that the crew of *Virginia* expected to lose.

    C is the best choice because *Virginia* had handily defeated two of the Union's vessels the day before it encountered *Monitor*. Without the arrival of *Monitor*, the Union's blockade would probably have been weakened significantly, at the least.

30. **(F)** In lines 40-41, the passage identifies Norfolk as the location of the naval base from which *Virginia* set sail. Thus, F is correct.

(Ergotism)

31. **(B)** The passage presented Linnda R. Caporael's hypothesis of what really happened in Salem to sparked the witch hunt and trials. The passage then presents a refutation of Linnda Caporael's hypothesis. That is why B works.

    A is incorrect because the author is not using the passage to show how simple it is to refute an argument. It is never mentioned that it was easy for Spanos and Gottlieb to refute Caporael's hypothesis. C is incorrect because the passage does not prove that the outbreaks by the three girls were caused by a food item. In fact, based on the passage alone, it is inconclusive what triggered the girls' outbursts. D is incorrect; the passage does nothing to urge readers to be cautious about what they eat. E is also similarly incorrect—the passage does not warn against jumping to conclusions.

32. **(G)** Lines 17-19 indicate that ergot was very common. In fact, it was so common that people thought it was a natural part of the grains or crops that it grew on. It can be assumed that the people didn't believe ergot to be toxic, since they thought it was safe to eat.

    F is incorrect because it is contradictory to what's suggested by the passage. H is incorrect because ergot's winter-time fate, or what the people of Salem believed to be ergot's winter-time fate, is not discussed in the passage. J is incorrect for a similar reason. While rye was Salem's staple grain in the summer months, and ergot grew on rye, there is nothing to indicate that the people of Salem believed ergot grew on rye only in the summertime. K is also unsupported by the passage. It is impossible to know whether the people of Salem Village could have cleaned ergot if they wanted to.

33. **(D)** The crux of Spanos and Gottlieb's argument is that records of gangrenous ergotism were never found. Ergot causes either gangrenous or convulsive ergotism. Which type afflicts a victim depends on whether his or her

levels of vitamin A. If the victim does not have enough vitamin A, convulsive ergotism will manifest, whereas gangrenous ergotism will manifest if the victim does have enough vitamin A. This means that the consumption of ergot results in one form of ergotism or the other.

Therefore, if ergotism was a problem in Salem, there should've been some records left of gangrenous ergotism afflicting the people of Salem, but no such records were found. D would weaken Spanos and Gottlieb's argument because it attacks their assumption that people would have recorded instances of gangrenous ergotism and is therefore the correct choice. The other choices are incorrect because they do not attack the core assumption that Spanos and Gottlieb make: that instances of either form of ergotism would have been recorded.

34. **(K)** Lines 4-6 provide the text for the correct answer. They list screaming, throwing objects, body contorting, and uttering sounds as the behaviors the three Salem girls exhibited. Frothing at the mouth was not one of the symptoms of bewitchment that the girls displayed, so K is the correct answer.

35. **(A)** A is the correct answer because in paragraph 2 (lines 13-23) ergot is described as toxic and it is this toxicity that Caporael believed caused the Salem girls' peculiar behavior. B is incorrect; it cannot be inferred that the effects of ergot can last months. It may be more accurate to say that ergot can survive for months, but that is not what this choice states. There is no indication that the Salem girls displayed "bewitched" behavior for months. C is incorrect. Vitamin A may protect against convulsive ergotism, but it does not protect against gangrenous ergotism (lines 36-39). D is incorrect. It is not stated or suggested by the passage that exposure to toxic substances typically results in death. This may be accurate, but it cannot be inferred. E is incorrect. The passage suggests in lines 32-36 that Salem Village had regular access to foods high in vitamin A.

(Animal Morality)

36. **(H)** This passage draws various comparisons between lions and hyenas but ultimately focuses on societal perceptions of each animal and why it may be unfair to judge animals according to human standards. H is best reflects this. The other choices are too narrow in scope to be the correct choice. Moreover, the other choices also use morally prejudicial terms, when the point of the passage is to promote fairness and objectivity towards animal behavioral patterns.

37. **(E)** The passage suggests in lines 24-27 that a lion can only sprint in short bursts because its heart makes up a very small percentage of its bodyweight. E is therefore the correct answer. The other choices cannot be inferred from the passage. For instance, there is no way to know if lions would hunt up to 95% of their food if they had bigger hearts, so we can rule choice A out. Similarly, there is no way to justify or prove the statements made in B, C, and D.

38. **(J)** Lines 34-36 indicate that lions have been viewed as symbols of regality, strength, ferocity, and bravery. Humility is not listed, thus making J the correct answer.

39. **(B)** The correct answer here is B. In lines 20-21, the passage states that the lion is indisputably an apex predator. The word "apex" means "top." A is wrong because lines 41-43 tell that it is obvious that we ascribe different sentiments to lions than we do to hyenas but that it is not as obvious why we do. C is incorrect because the author wants people not to judge animals negatively; there is nothing to indicate that he wants animals to abide by humanity's code of ethics (lines 44-48).

D is incorrect. The passages makes no mention of animals' ability to experience emotions; thus, it is cannot be determined whether the author would agree with the statement. E is incorrect because hyenas are often vilified (lines 37-41); it is not apparent from the passage that hyenas are popular in some cultures.

40. **(J)** Lines 10-14 answer this question. The paucity of readily available water and an abundance of sun are what make for brutal living conditions in the dry season in Africa. J is the choice that properly reflects this.

F is incorrect because there isn't a shortage of sun in the dry season. G is incorrect because the passage does not attribute the brutality of the dry season to a lack of prey. The statements made in H and K have nothing to do with the brutality of the dry season in Africa.

(Las Vegas)

41. **(C)** This passage is about how the city of Las Vegas came to be, so C is the correct answer. The other choices refer to points made but do not reflect the passage's main idea.

42. **(G)** Lines 12-19 establish the Mexican Cession as the victory prize for the United States for winning the Mexican-American War. G is therefore the correct answer. The Mexican Cession included Nevada, where Las Vegas is situated, but it is not implied by the passage that Las Vegas would become the most important city in the Mexican Cession, so F is not correct. H is not correct because the passage indicates that the United States won the war. J and K are not correct because they cannot be inferred from the passage.

43. **(E)** Lines 33-36 state that Brigham Young recalled his missionaries from Las Vegas because of a power struggle that broke out between Bringhurst and Jones. E is therefore the correct choice. The statements made by the other choices are not supported.

44. **(F)** Lines 37-41 and 43-47 provide the context for the answer to this question. Las Vegas served as a missionary post, so G is not correct. H is incorrect because Las Vegas was a railroad town. J is incorrect because Las Vegas first served as agricultural farmland. K

is incorrect because Las Vegas became known as the "Entertainment Capital of the World," once gambling was legalized.

45. **(E)** E is the correct answer. Modern-day Las Vegas is reputed for its entertainment. In lines 43-47, the legalization of gambling is attributed to Las Vegas's metamorphosis into Sin City and world's Entertainment Capital.

The other choices are incorrect. While they bring up Las Vegas's origins, those events did not contribute to people's contemporary perception of Las Vegas.

(Rudolf Andersen, Jr.)

46. **(H)** The passage is about the actions Major Rudolf Andersen took on behalf of the United States and the consequences and aftermath of his actions. Specifically, Major Andersen's death served as a solemn reminder just how close the Cold War was to becoming an all-out war. H is therefore correct.

F is incorrect. Major Andersen was a hero, but the main idea of the passage is not why he deserved the medals he was awarded. G is incorrect because it is draws a conclusion that is not supported by the passage. J is incorrect because it is not supported by the passage. While the passage does mention that death can remind us why peace is necessary, it does not suggest that lives must be sacrificed in order to achieve world peace. K may be a correct statement, but that is not the main idea of this passage.

47. **(D)** The support for the answer to this question can be found in lines 13-19. The passage states that Operation Brass Knob was a series of high-altitude missions over Cuba involving reconnaissance airplanes. Major Andersen was one of the pilots and came back with photographs proving the Soviet Union's involvement Cuba's nuclear armament. D is therefore correct.

A is not supported by the passage. B is incorrect because, until Major Andersen's death, there had been no casualties of the Cold War. C is tempting, but it is not supported enough by the passage to make it the correct choice. E is incorrect because the operation's purpose wasn't to assess the U-2's effectiveness.

48. **(K)** In lines 33-37, the passage states that Kennedy did not order a retaliation because he did not believe that Khrushchev would have ordered an unarmed reconnaissance aircraft to be shot down, given the tenuousness of the situation. Thus, K is the correct answer. The other choices are unsupported by the passage.

49. **(C)** A and C are the best two answers, based on the passage. In lines 26-29, the passage indicates that the shrapnel from an exploding surface-to-air missile killed Major Andersen. It does not indicate whether the missile first hit Major Andersen or his aircraft. As a result, C is better. B, D, and E are not mentioned in the passage. The facts presented in E are accurate, however, which may make E appealing to those who know the full story. Even if the passage had mentioned the facts of E, E still would not be correct. If Major Andersen had not flown that particular day, he would have perhaps survived the Cold War, but his flying did not cause his death.

50. **(G)** In the last paragraph, from lines 42-49, the passage states that Major Andersen was the first to be awarded the Air Force Cross, the service's highest distinction after the Medal of Honor. This means the Air Force Cross is the second highest distinction that an airman in the Air Force can earn; G properly reflects this. F is incorrect because the Air Force Cross is more prestigious than other medals as well. H and K are inaccurate in saying that the Air Force Cross is the highest medal than an airman can earn. J is incorrect. The passage does not state when or why the Air Force Cross was created.

MATH EXPLANATIONS ▶

Answer Explanations – Mathematics
Practice Test 2

51. **(E)** One way to solve this problem is to eliminate the incorrect answer choices, until you arrive at the correct answer choice.

A is incorrect because y may be greater in magnitude than x, which would make $x + y$ negative. B is incorrect because a negative number minus a positive number will always be negative. C is incorrect because if the absolute value of y is greater than the value of x, then y^2 will be greater than x^2. D is incorrect because $(x - y)^2 = x^2 - 2xy + y^2$. The only way D could be correct is if at least one of the variables is 0. This leaves E as the correct answer.

E is correct because a positive number minus a negative number will always be positive, since subtracting a negative number gives the same value as adding the absolute value of the negative number.

52. **(J)** To solve this problem, first convert all of the percentages to decimal numbers:

$20\% = 0.2$, and $18\% = .18$

Next, do the required multiplications, remembering that the word "of" in mathematics refers to multiplication:

$V = 0.2 \times W$

$W = 0.18 \times X$

Next, substitute $0.18X$ in for W:

$V = 0.2 \times (0.18X) = 0.036X$, which means that $V = 3.6\%$ of X.

53. **(B)** First distribute the 4 across the left side of the equation and the 2 across the right side of the equation:

$12x - 20 = 2y + 6$

Next, subtract 6 from both sides to get $2y$.

$2y = 12x - 26$

Divide by 2 to solve for y:

$y = 6x - 13$

54. **(H)** If a prime number is squared, the resulting number will have 3 factors: 1, the prime number, and itself.

For instance, try squaring 13, which is a prime number:

$13^2 = 169$

The factors of 169 are: 1, 13, 169

Interesting Fact: All perfect squares have an odd number of factors.

55. **(C)** To solve this problem, make sure to flip the fraction in the middle and multiply:

$$7.8 \div \frac{13}{2} \times 8 \ = \ \frac{78}{10} \times \frac{2}{13} \times 8$$

$$\frac{\overset{6}{\cancel{78}}}{\underset{5}{\cancel{10}}} \times \frac{\overset{1}{\cancel{2}}}{\underset{1}{\cancel{13}}} \times 8 \ = \ \frac{48}{5} \ = \ 9\frac{3}{5} \ = \ 9.6$$

56. **(G)** For the sake of simplicity, assign variables for Reggie and Ramon's ages, such as:

R = Reggie's age, and M = Ramon's age. Then set up equations with the given information:

R = M + 13

R + 9 = 2(M + 9) → R + 9 = 2M + 18

Subtract 9 from each side to get R:

R = 2M + 9

Substitute 2M + 9 for R to get:

2M + 9 = M + 13 → M = 4

---

57. **(A)** LM = 1 − (⁻6) = 7; LN = 5 − (⁻6) = 11

The ratio of LM to LN is therefore 7 to 11 or 7 : 11.

---

58. **(J)** The best way to approach this problem is to pick a value of x that would give the expression of $x + 2$ a remainder of 5 when divided by 6.

One such value of x is 9.

$2x + 2 = 20$, which gives a remainder of 2 when divided by 6.

Try this with other viable values of x, and you will get the same result.

---

59. **(A)** This problem is one of simplification.

$$\frac{m+n}{\cancel{m}\,\cancel{n}}\left[\left(\frac{n^{\cancel{2}}}{\cancel{n}}\right)\left(\frac{\cancel{m}^{\cancel{2}}}{-n-m}\right)\right] =$$

It should be noted that $(m + n) = {}^{-}(-n - m)$. Thus, when these terms are divided, they simplify to ⁻1, and the final answer is ⁻n.

60. **(G)** The best way to solve this problem is to compare each of the answer choices.

F: From hours 1 to 2, the bacteria count went from 100 to 150, representing a growth of 50, or 50%.

G: From hours 2 to 3, the bacteria count went from 150 to 250, representing a growth of 100, or 66.67%.

H: From hours 3 to 5, the bacteria count went from 250 to 400, representing a growth of 150, or 60%.

J: From hours 4 to 6, the bacteria count went from 300 to approximately 475, representing a growth of 175, or 58.33%.

K: From hours 5 to 7, the bacteria count went from 400 to 500, representing a growth of 100, or 25%.

Thus, G shows the greatest percent growth.

---

61. **(A)** To solve this problem, the area of the circle must be subtracted from the area of the trapezoid.

The area of a trapezoid is: $\frac{1}{2} \times h \times (b_1 + b_2)$

In this case, the height (h) is 6 cm, or the diameter of the circle inscribed in the trapezoid.

Trapezoid ABCD's area is $\frac{1}{2} \times 6(12 + 8)$, or 60 cm².

The circle's area is 9π cm².

The shaded region's area is $60 - 9\pi$ cm². By factoring out 3 from each term of the solution, we get $3(20 - 3\pi)$ cm².

62. **(J)** First, distribute the 3 on the left side of the equation.

$$6x - 15y + 4 = 7y - 5x + 37$$

Since we're looking to find x, bring all of the x terms to one side and everything else to the other.

$$11x = 22y + 33$$

Dividing each side by 11, we get x:
$$x = 2y + 3$$

63. **(E)** If Gina is g years old, then Mina is $g + 8$ years old. 13 years ago, Mina would have been $(g + 8) - 13$, or $g - 5$, years old.

64. **(J)** To solve this problem, first realize that triangle BDE is similar to triangle ABC. That means that every corresponding part of the two triangles has the same ratio. Thus, we can reason that the height of triangle BDE is half of that of ABC, since the base of triangle BDE (8 cm) is half that of triangle ABC (16 cm). Also, we should realize that the area of triangle ABC is the sum of the areas of triangle BDE and trapezoid ADEC.

From the area of ADEC, which is 72 cm², we can find the height of the trapezoid.

$$72 = \frac{1}{2} \times h \times (b_1 + b_2)$$

$$= \frac{1}{2} \times h \times (8 + 16)$$

$$= 12h \rightarrow h = 6 \text{ cm}$$

Trapezoid ADEC's height is equal to the height of triangle BDE, since the height of triangle ABC is twice that of triangle BDE. Triangle BDE's area is: $\frac{1}{2} \times 6 \times 8 = 24$ cm².

Thus, the total area of triangle ABC is: $(72 + 24)$ cm² $= 96$ cm²

65. **(C)** There is a much more efficient method to solving this problem than squaring the whole number. Since only the tens place is what we're looking for, you just need to square 87 to find the tens place.

$$87 \times 87 = 7,569$$

This indicates that 6 is in the tens place of the square of 1,365,787.

66. **(G)** Alex spent c cents. Sam spent $c + 4$ dollars, which is equivalent to $100c + 400$ cents.

Together, they spent:

$$c + (100c + 400) = 101c + 400 \text{ cents}$$

67. **(D)** If a car travels 7,065 feet after one of its tires spins 1,500 times, the circumference of the tire can be found by dividing 7,065 by 1,500:

$$7,065 \div 1,500 = 4.71 \text{ feet.}$$

Divide 4.71 feet by 3.14 (an approximation of π):

$$4.71 \div 3.14 = 1.5 \text{ feet}$$

Convert 1.5 feet to inches:

$$1.5 \text{ feet} \times 12 \text{ inches/feet} = 18 \text{ inches}$$

68. **(K)** First substitute 6 in for r:

$$\frac{7(q - 6)}{5}$$

Because the above expression is a positive integer, we know that $q - 6$ must be a multiple of 5. The smallest value of $q - 6$ is therefore 5. Thus, the smallest possible q is 11.

69. (C) Tammy's average score across 4 tests was 73; the sum of Tammy's scores across the tests was therefore $73 \times 4 = 292$.

The sum of the three known test scores is $56 + 67 + 91 = 214$.

The last test score is then $292 - 214 = 78$.

70. (G) If the ratio of girls to boys is 8 : 5, that means that there the total number of boys and girls is a multiple of 13. And, indeed, we see that the total number of students is 78, which is 6×13. This means that the number of students can be broken down as follows:

Girls: $6 \times 8 = 48$
Boys: $6 \times 5 = 30$

As we can see, there are 18 fewer boys than girls ($48 - 30 = 18$).

71. (E) $\sqrt{5^2} + \sqrt{12^2} = 5 + 12 = 17$

$\sqrt{5^2 + 12^2} = \sqrt{169} = 13$

The difference is therefore $17 - 13 = 4$.

72. (G) Set up the following equation:

$\$2.50x + \$3.33y = \$32.48$

Note that the staplers cannot result in a price that ends in an 8. This means that the number of hole punchers has to be 6, 16, 26, etc. We see that the only possible value of y is 6 because that is the only one that fits. 16×3.33, for instance, is 53.28.

If $y = 6$, then the hole punchers cost $\$19.98$. This indicates that the staplers cost $\$12.50$, which means $x = 5$.

To find the total number of items Grover purchased, we do $x + y = 11$.

73. (B) To solve this problem, we first plug in 8 for s and perform the operation:

$\dfrac{8 - 16}{4} = -2$

Then we plug 6 in for r and do the operation again:

$\dfrac{6 - 2(-2)}{4} = \dfrac{10}{4} = 2.5$

74. (H) To calculate the probability of Ricky picking up either a blue or yellow crayon, first determine the respective probabilities of him picking the blue crayon and of him picking the yellow crayon.

$P(B) = \dfrac{8}{20}$

$P(Y) = \dfrac{1}{20}$ because there is 1 yellow crayon:
$20 - (8 + 5 + 6) = 1$

The probability that Ricky will pick either a blue or yellow crayon is $P(B) + P(Y)$:

$\dfrac{8}{20} + \dfrac{1}{20} = \dfrac{9}{20} = 0.45$

75. (A) Distribute $5z$ across the terms of the polynomial enclosed in the parentheses:

$5z(6w - 7) = 30zw - 35z$

76. (G) If 4 workers can build 6 houses in 540 hours, then 1 worker can build 6 houses in $4 \times 540 = 2,160$ hours, or 90 days.

To build 6 houses in 10 days, then there needs to be $1 \times 9 = 9$ workers. Thus, 5 additional workers are needed.

77. **(E)** Quentin's average time across 5 trials was 4.62 seconds. This means that the sum of Quentin's times across the trials was $4.62 \times 5 = 23.1$ seconds.

The sum of the four known trial times is $4.7 + 4.61 + 4.65 + 4.59 = 18.55$ seconds

The last trial time is then $23.1 - 18.55 = 4.55$ seconds.

Arranging the times in order from least to greatest, we get: 4.55, 4.59, 4.61, 4.65, and 4.7. The median is therefore 4.61 seconds.

The difference between the final time and the median time is $4.61 - 4.55 = 0.06$.

---

78. **(J)** To find the sum of the set of numbers, you should *not* try to add all the numbers manually. Look for an addition pattern.

$2 + 204 = 206$; $4 + 202 = 206$; $6 + 200 = 206$

From 2 to 204, counting by 2's, there are 102 numbers, which means that 51 pairs of numbers adding up to 206 can be made. The correct answer is therefore $51 \times 206 = 10,506$.

---

79. **(D)** If 2 cubits = 1 yard, and there is ¼ of a yard in a span, then 4 spans = 1 yard. That means 2 cubits = 4 spans, and 1 cubit is equal to 2 times a span.

---

80. **(K)** First, divide 5,446 by 386 to find how many fish each person in the village receives and the remainder.

$5,446 \div 386 = 14 \text{ R}42$

The difference between the remainder and the fish that each person received is:

$42 - 14 = 28$

81. **(C)** Convert all of the mixed numbers to improper fractions because it's easier to deal with improper fractions for multiplication and division problems:

$$5\frac{7}{13} = \frac{72}{13}; \quad 2\frac{8}{9} = \frac{26}{9}$$

Multiplying the two improper fractions will yield the number of miles Yasmin ran:

$$\frac{\overset{8}{\cancel{72}}}{\underset{1}{\cancel{13}}} \times \frac{\overset{2}{\cancel{26}}}{\underset{1}{\cancel{9}}} = 16 \text{ miles}$$

---

82. **(G)** First, find 80% of $48.24:

$0.8 \times 48.24 = 38.592$

In order to find the lowest price Jeremy can sell each of the 5 watermelons, divide 38.592 by 5:

$38.592 \div 5 = 7.7184$.

Rounding up to the nearest cent, to ensure he makes back at least $38.592, we get $7.72.

---

83. **(C)** Write an equation to solve this problem:

$x + (x + 2) + (x + 4) + (x + 6) + (x + 8) = 155$

Simplifying the equation, we get:

$5x + 20 = 155$

$5x = 135$

$x = 27$

Since the largest number is $x + 8$, the correct answer is 35.

84. **(G)** This problem is simpler than it looks. Take away the unlabeled transversal (a line that goes through two or more parallel lines) with the positive slope. After this line is taken away, the only marked angles that are left should be 62° and $x°$. These angles are *alternate exterior angles*, meaning that they have the same angle measure.

In other words, the 73° is irrelevant to solving this problem.

---

85. **(B)** A has coordinates of (‾3, 2), while B has coordinates of (3, ‾4). Use the distance formula to find the length of segment AB.

$$\text{Distance} = \sqrt{(x_2 - x_1)^2 + (y_2 - y_1)^2}$$

$$= \sqrt{(3 - {}^-3)^2 + ({}^-4 - 2)^2}$$

$$= \sqrt{72} = 6\sqrt{2}$$

---

86. **(F)** First, find the number of red straws:

$$P(\text{R}) = \frac{\text{red straw}}{\text{total straws}} = 12.5\% = 0.125$$

$$0.125 = \frac{1}{8} = \frac{\text{R}}{40}$$

Solving for R, we get 5.

The number of non-red straws that need to be added in order to make the probability of drawing a red straw can be determined:

$$P(\text{R}) = \frac{\text{red straw}}{\text{total straws}} = \frac{5}{40 + N} = 4\% = 0.04$$

$$\frac{4}{100} = \frac{5}{40 + N} \;\rightarrow\; 500 = 4N + 160$$

$$4N = 340 \;\rightarrow\; N = 85$$

87. **(E)** First, simplify the fractions by multiplying them out:

$$\frac{\cancel{3}^{1}}{\cancel{4}_{1}} K \times \frac{\cancel{20}^{5}}{\cancel{21}^{7}} = \frac{5}{7} K$$

This means that K must be 7, so that the 7s cancel out and leave an integer value.

---

88. **(J)** To solve this problem, cross out pairs of numbers, starting from the lowest and highest numbers, i.e., 68 and 103 is the first pair you should cross out, until you arrive at the middle number, which is the median.

Here, there are two middle numbers, 78 and 80. In the case of two middle numbers, take the average of the two:

$$(78 + 80)/2 = 79$$

---

89. **(D)** Set up several equations to solve this problem:

$$C + F = 5,400$$

$$F = 2C \;\rightarrow\; 3C = 5,400 \;\rightarrow\; C = 1,800$$

If there are 1,800 canaries, there are 3,600 finches on the island. Set up another equation to determine how many male and female finches there are:

$$F = F_f + F_m = 3,600$$

$$F_f = 1.5 \times F_m \;\rightarrow\; 2.5 \times F_m = 3,600$$

$$F_m = 1,440$$

Thus, there are $1,800 + 1,440 = 3,240$ total birds on the island that aren't female finches.

90. **(J)** An isosceles right triangle is one whose side lengths (not including the hypotenuse) are the same. Furthermore, if the side length is x, then the hypotenuse is $x\sqrt{2}$.

In this case, the triangle's hypotenuse is $7\sqrt{2}$ cm, so the side length is 7 cm. If one of these sides is shared with a square, then the square's side length is also 7 cm; the area of the square would be 49 cm^2.

---

91. **(E)** Use the process of elimination to arrive at the correct answer:

A is incorrect because $Y(Y-1)$ would be even, since Y is even.

B is incorrect because Y/2 may be odd (or not even an integer), and an odd number plus an even number is odd.

C is incorrect because $Y+1$ doesn't have to be prime. For instance, if Y = 8, Y + 1 = 9, which is not prime.

D is incorrect. Try substituting 2 for Y. 2Y + 1 = 5, which is not divisible by 3.

E is correct because $Y-1$ is odd, and if it's squared, that means you'd be multiplying an odd integer with an odd integer, which will always result in an odd integer.

---

92. **(F)** If ½-inch on a map represents 75 miles, then 1 mile would be represented by:

$$1 \text{ mile} = \frac{1}{2} \div 75 = \frac{1}{150} \text{ inches}$$

Then, find how many square inches on a map would represent 1 square mile:

$$1 \text{ mi.}^2 = \frac{1}{(150)^2} \text{ in.}^2$$

$$100 \text{ mi.}^2 = \frac{100}{(150)^2} \text{ in.}^2 = \frac{100}{150 \times 150} \text{ in.}^2$$

$$\frac{100}{150 \times 150} = \frac{100}{(15 \times 10) \times (15 \times 10)} = \frac{100}{15^2 \times 100}$$

Cancel out the 100s:

$$\frac{1}{15^2} \text{ in.}^2$$

---

93. **(A)** The volume of a box is $l \times w \times h$. But notice that the answer is in cubic feet. As such, we must make the necessary conversions in order to arrive at the correct answer.

Length: 10 in. $= \dfrac{5}{6}$ ft.

Width: 0.75 ft. $= \dfrac{3}{4}$ ft.

Height: 4 in. $= \dfrac{1}{3}$ ft.

Multiply all of the fractions together:

$$\frac{5}{6} \times \frac{\cancel{3}}{4} \times \frac{1}{\cancel{3}} = \frac{5}{24} \text{ ft.}^3$$

---

94. **(H)** 1.0684 rounded to the nearest hundredth is 1.07, which is g.

$$1.0684 + 1.07 = 2.1384$$

---

95. **(A)** By plugging in 2 for x and 3 for y, you should end up with:

$$(2^2 + 3^2)(^-3^2 + 2^2) = (4+9)(^-9+4)$$

$$(13)(^-5) = ^-65$$

96. **(H)** Draw a diagram to assist you solving this problem:

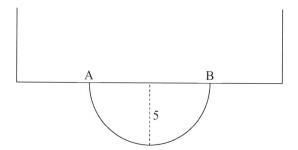

The dotted line represents the rope. Because the barn wall is longer than the diameter of the circle that could otherwise be created by the dog, if the wall weren't there, and the dog is tied to the middle of the barn, we need only worry about the straight line distance between points A and B and the half-circumference that exists between the points.

The half-circumference is $\frac{1}{2} \times 2 \times 5 \times \pi$, or 5π, feet. Line segment AB is simply the diameter of the circle and has a length of 10 feet. Thus, the perimeter of the area that the dog can roam is $10 + 5\pi$ feet.

---

97. **(E)** First, find the number of white roses:

(T)otal = (R)ed + (P)ink + (W)hite

$35 = 18 + 10 + W$

$W = 35 - (18 + 10) = 7$

Next, find the ratio of white roses to the total number of roses:

$$\frac{W}{T} = \frac{7}{35} = \frac{1}{5}$$

This means that, out of 1,000 roses, the best estimate of white roses would be:

$$\frac{W}{1,000} = \frac{1}{5} \rightarrow 5W = 1,000 \rightarrow W = 200$$

98. **(G)** The third vertex can be either directly above or below the center (halfway) of the edge whose vertices we are given.

Find the height of the equilateral triangle to solve this problem by cutting it in half, to get a 30-60-90 special right triangle:

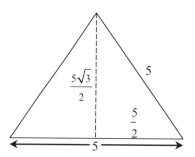

This indicates that the coordinates of the third vertex of the equilateral triangle in our problem are either:

$$\left(\frac{5}{2}, \frac{5\sqrt{3}}{2} \right) \quad \text{or} \quad \left(\frac{5}{2}, -\frac{5\sqrt{3}}{2} \right)$$

---

99. **(B)** If you know the formula to calculate the interior angles of a polygon, you could use the formula of $180° \times (n - 2)$, where n the number of sides of the polygon. Plugging in 12 for n would lead to $180° \times 10 = 1,800°$.

Otherwise, you could calculate $12 \times 180° = 2,160°$ (for 12 triangles and 180° per triangle). Then you would subtract 360° from this result to get the correct answer because the tips of all the triangles form the number of degrees in a circle.

---

100. **(J)** First, realize that 1 yard = 3 feet, so 1 $yd^2 = 9$ ft^2. This means 10 $yd^2 = 90$ ft^2, or that 1 gallon of paint covers 90 ft^2.

To find how many cans of paint need to be opened, do $2,000 \div 90$ is 22 R20. Thus, 23 cans must be opened to cover the entire 2,000 ft^2.

SHSAT
TJHSST EDITION

TEST KEY 3

Answer Key – Test 3

VERBAL

SCRAMBLED PARAGRAPHS

Paragraph 1
UQRTS

Paragraph 2
SUQRT

Paragraph 3
QTSUR

Paragraph 4
QSURT

Paragraph 5
RSQUT

LOGICAL REASONING

11. E
12. K
13. E
14. K
15. D
16. H
17. B
18. F
19. B
20. J
21. E
22. J
23. C
24. F
25. A

READING

26. K
27. D
28. J
29. C
30. G
31. E
32. G
33. C
34. F
35. A
36. J
37. B
38. H
39. C
40. K
41. B
42. K
43. A
44. G
45. D
46. F
47. E
48. J
49. A
50. H

MATH ANSWERS ▶

Answer Key – Test 3

MATHEMATICS

51. E	**76.** F
52. G	**77.** D
53. A	**78.** J
54. K	**79.** B
55. C	**80.** G
56. J	**81.** D
57. A	**82.** K
58. J	**83.** E
59. E	**84.** J
60. G	**85.** C
61. B	**86.** K
62. G	**87.** B
63. A	**88.** G
64. H	**89.** B
65. E	**90.** H
66. H	**91.** B
67. D	**92.** F
68. G	**93.** A
69. D	**94.** G
70. K	**95.** D
71. E	**96.** K
72. H	**97.** E
73. A	**98.** F
74. F	**99.** C
75. C	**100.** J

VERBAL EXPLANATIONS ▶

Answer Explanations – Verbal
Practice Test 3

SCRAMBLED PARAGRAPHS

Paragraph 1 (UQRTS)

The lead sentence introduces intel as a critical component of national security.

Sentence U comes after the lead because it introduces the Central Intelligence Agency, or CIA, as the agency responsible for gathering and analyzing intel. Q comes after U because it introduces what happened prior to the establishment of the CIA. R follows Q because it follows up on what is stated in Q. T follows R, which introduces the Office of Strategic Services, by stating that the creation of OSS didn't satisfactorily solve the problem of intelligence decentralization. Finally, S comes last and makes it apparent why a central intelligence agency was needed.

Note: It may be tempting to pick U after S chronologically, but it makes more sense for U to come before Q because U introduces the CIA. Without U, Q wouldn't have a proper reference point, and the paragraph would become illogical.

Tip: Make a cluster with R, T, and S because they focus on OSS. Also make a cluster with U and Q. In this way, the paragraph becomes much easier to unscramble. Between U coming after the lead sentence or R coming after the lead, it should be apparent that U does.

Paragraph 2 (SUQRT)

The opening sentence starts the paragraph with a discussion of the Great Wall of China as one of the most ambitious manmade undertakings. Sentence S comes after the lead because it is about the start of the Great Wall's construction. U comes after S because it further details what Emperor Qin did to commence construction of the Great Wall. Q comes after U because it discusses the end of the Qin Dynasty.

R comes after Q. After the collapse of the Qin Dynasty, the Great Wall fell into a state of disrepair. Furthermore, the Wall lost much of its militaristic significance, especially after Genghis Kahn took over China. T follows R because it closes the paragraph with a discussion of how the Ming Dynasty resurrected the Great Wall project.

Tip: This paragraph proceeded in chronological order, so that is the key to successfully unscrambling this paragraph. Also, it is possible to make a 3-sentence cluster of SUQ and a 2-sentence pair of RT.

Paragraph 3 (QTSUR)

The opening sentence indicates that the paragraph will be about lacrosse. It introduces some statistics, as well. Q comes after the lead because it further discusses the comparison of lacrosse with other sports made by the lead sentence. Q also informs us that lacrosse is North America's oldest indigenous sport.

T follows Q because it begins the discussion on the origination of lacrosse as a sport. S follows T because it explains the role of lacrosse in Native American tribes. U follows S because it provides more details about lacrosse games, as an extension of S. R follows U and concludes the paragraph by ushering in the potential for a discussion of modern lacrosse.

Tip: Like the previous paragraph, this paragraph proceeds chronologically. As long as you remember that, you should have no problem. A relatively easy cluster to make for this paragraph is TSU.

Paragraph 4 (QSURT)

The lead sentence states that ladybugs can be a valuable resource and aide for farmers and agriculturalists.

Q comes after the lead to describe the ladybug's appearance and to explain how these beetles can help farmers. S comes after Q and explains that ladybugs were in fact imported from Asia because of how helpful they can be to farmers. U comes after S to provide context for the word "voracious," as it is used in sentence S. R follows U and explains that the ladybug will continue eating bugs such as aphids even past its larval stage.

Finally, the last sentence is T because it wraps up the paragraph and introduces another possible topic of discussion: the damage to the ecosystems ladybugs have caused.

Note: It may be tempting to choose T after S because S mentions importing ladybugs, and T mentions the ramifications of the importation of ladybugs. T does not come after S, however, because it would disrupt the flow of the paragraph for the sentences that follow T. If T came after S, then the sentence following T should be about the damage to the ecosystem that ladybugs have caused.

Paragraph 5 (RSQUT)

The lead sentence alerts us to the fact that *Sesame Street* is a children's television phenomenon.

Sentence R comes after the introductory sentence because it discusses the show's conception. S comes after R to further explain why and how Joan Ganz planned to design the show. Q comes after S because it is connected by the mention of a fun but educational program.

U comes next, after Q, and recites the launch of the first airing of *Sesame Street*. T comes after U to indicate how much of a success the show was, even from the beginning. Furthermore, T talks about the impact *Sesame Street* has had on its viewers.

Tip: Here, the easy clusters to make are RSQ and UT. By making these two clusters, unscrambling the paragraph should become much easier. It makes much more sense for R to come after the lead than for U to come after the lead; in fact, it wouldn't make any sense if U came after the lead. Thus, the correct answer is indeed RSQUT.

LOGICAL REASONING ▶

AE

LOGICAL REASONING

11. **(E)** This question requires you to work with conditional statements and their contrapositives.

    The first statement is: If I am full, I will not eat. The contrapositive of this statement is: If I eat, I am not full.

    The second statement is: If I eat, I will drink soda. The contrapositive of this statement is: If I do not drink soda, I do not eat.

    E is the only proper conclusion that can be drawn from the conditional statements and their contrapositives. A is not a proper conclusion because it requires the statement "If I drink soda, I do/will eat," but that is not a valid statement that can be drawn from the two given conditional statements. This also eliminates B. C is not a proper conclusion because it is possible to be hungry without eating. D is incorrect because it is possible to not eat but not be full.

12. **(K)** Everyone in Puntsville is good at kicking a football. Some of these people can kick a field goal from 60 yards away. These people can also run a 5-minute mile, since everyone who can kick a 60-yard field goal can. Thus, the correct answer is K.

    J is tricky. Common sense may dictate that anyone who can kick a 60-yard field goal is also good at kicking a football. Strictly based on the facts of this problem, it is erroneous to correlate being good at kicking a football and being able to kick a 60-yard field goal. For instance, it may be possible to kick a 60-yard field goal by luck. That doesn't necessarily mean that the person is good at kicking. "Good" hasn't been defined.

13. **(E)** There are 51 cops and robbers sitting around a in a circle. Cops always tell the truth, while robbers always lie. If one person says, "There is a cop to my right," while everyone else says, "A robber is to my right,"

then that means the cops and robbers are sitting around the table, alternating between cops and robbers, except for the one person who says a cop is sitting to his right. This means that there will either be 26 cops and 25 robbers or 26 robbers and 25 cops. It is not known which one is true, however. Therefore, the answer is E.

Tip: Try drawing out an alternating circular pattern with a smaller odd number of cops and robbers, if you're having a hard time grasping the solution to the problem.

14. **(K)** This problem is one of logical comparison. The only logical conclusion that can be drawn is K because nothing other than acceleration is being compared. If a cheetah can accelerate faster than a Ferrari Enzo, which is one of the fastest accelerating cars in the world, to 60 miles per hour, then the cheetah can accelerate at least as fast as one of the world's fastest accelerating cars, from 0 to 60 miles per hour.

    F is incorrect because it would be able to beat the Enzo in a race that required the cheetah to hit 60 miles per hour. G is incorrect because there isn't enough information in the problem to support it. H is also similarly incorrect. J is also incorrect because there isn't enough information to support it, even if it seems to be a common sense choice. It is entirely possible that until 30 miles per hour, the Enzo is faster, but between 30 miles per hour and 60 miles per hour, the cheetah accelerates faster. Keep in mind that only information from the problem may be used to draw conclusions.

15. **(D)** The best approach for this problem is to draw a chart or diagram. Initially, before much deduction, we can draw a chart:

	First in Closet
1.	Jacket –
2.	– Violet
3.	
4.	
5.	– Magenta
	Last in Closet

After considering that the sundress is turquois, we know that the jacket cannot be turquois. Thus, turquois, which comes before pink, comes immediately after violet. The gown comes immediately before the sundress, and we can thus arrive at the chart below:

First in Closet

1.	Jacket –
2.	Gown – Violet
3.	Sundress – Turquois
4.	– Pink
5.	– Magenta

Last in Closet

If the blouse comes before the coat, that means that the blouse has to be pink and the coat has to be magenta. D is correct.

16. **(H)** This problem involves, at its core, a series of conditional statements, which can be rewritten as:

  5) M → ~B
  6) R → ~HF
  7) B → ~R
  8) B → ~HF

Note: ~ means "not." As such, the first conditional statement should be read, "If M, then not B." Of course that in itself is an abbreviated form of "If Shawna reads a mystery novel, she will not read a biography."

For simplicity, the last conditional statement was broken down into two. By looking at these conditional statements, it is possible to figure out the contrapositives.

  5) B → ~M
  6) HF → ~R
  7) R → ~B
  8) HF → ~B

From the above, it is possible to conclude that if Shawna reads a mystery in a given week, she could also read a historical fiction or romance novel, but not both. Thus, the correct answer choice is H.

17. **(B)** The best way to solve this is to draw out the possible pyramid formations, according to the information presented:

Possibility #1:

Top of Pyramid

1.	Carrie		
2.	Jake		Doug
3.	Bart	Pete	

Bottom of Pyramid

Possibility #2:

Top of Pyramid

1.	Carrie		
2.	Jake		Doug
3.		Bart	Pete

Bottom of Pyramid

Possibility #3:

Top of Pyramid

1.	Carrie		
2.	Jake		Doug
3.	Bart		Pete

Bottom of Pyramid

Based on these three possibilities, it is possible to deduce that there are actually three spots in the pyramid that Kirk could occupy. Even if Jake and Doug and Bart and Pete switched rows, Kirk could only occupy a space on the bottom row.

Note: This question is NOT asking for how many distinct pyramid formations could be made. If it were, then the correct answer would be 6.

18. **(F)** Here, the facts show that I am either the smartest kid or can read as much per week as the smartest kid can. This question may lead some people to believe that how many books one can read is the measure of smartness, but that's not necessarily true. Thus, F best expresses the correct answer. There is nothing to establish that I am the smartest kid in my school. Thus, G is incorrect. H is an improper

conclusion to draw based on the facts. If the reading speed is not what determines smartness, then both J and K are incorrect. In order for G, H, J, and K to work as answer choices, the facts must first have established that smartness is defined by the number of books a student can read. Because smartness has not been so defined, they are wrong choices.

19. **(B)** Here, the best strategy is to draw a diagram or chart.

First Animal Passed

1.	C			
2.	L			
3.	F	L		
4.		F	L	
5.			F	L
6.				F

Last Animal Passed

Based on the information, it is possible to figure out that there are 4 possible places where the lizard and fox could fit. And since this leaves three spaces open for the dog, bird, and squirrel, without any contradictions to the facts, the correct answer is B.

20. **(J)** At most, Yancy can walk to work 8 times in a span of 4 weeks, if he walks to work twice a week every week. This means that he can take the bus home at most 8 times, as well. At the very least, he can walk to work 4 times in 4 weeks because he has to walk to work at least once a week, which means he takes the bus home 4 times. Thus, the difference between the most number of times he can take the bus home and the least is $8 - 4 = 4$.

21. **(E)** If Mount Juneau is the tallest mountain in Peaksland, and Mount Yaro is taller than Juneau, then it is impossible for Yaro to be in Peaksland. As such, the correcet answer is E.

The other choices could be true, but aren't necessarily true. A is incorrect because it is possible for Yaro to be in Heightsland. B is incorrect because Yaro could be in Peaksland, as long as Yaro isn't taller than

any mountain in Heightsland. C is incorrect. Even if Mount Juneau is the tallest mountain in Peaksland, that does not automatically make Yaro a Heightsland mountain. D is incorrect because it is not known what Juneau's relative height is, compared to other Peaksland mountains.

22. **(J)** This question is best solved by drawing a table or diagram.

First to Bus

1.	Soleil
2.	
3.	
4.	Nancy
5.	Priscilla

Last to Bus

Based on the first and third facts, the above diagram can be constructed. Three students separate Priscilla and Soleil, who reached the bus first. Priscilla reached the bus immediately after Nancy did, so Nancy is fourth. That leaves the second fact, which states that Macy reached the bust immediately before Rita did. Thus, Macy is second and Rita is third. The correct order is therefore Soleil, Macy, Rita, Nancy, and Priscilla.

23. **(C)** Draw a diagram or chart to solve this problem. Be sure to keep track of the students and what their respective booths are about. Another thing to keep in mind is that by "smaller" and "bigger" numbers, the problem means that 1 is smaller than 5, 4 is bigger than 3, etc.

The facts show that both the ice cream and the music booths had bigger numbers than the stickers booth. And because Brandi was assigned to the ice cream booth, the biggest possible number for Brandi and her ice cream booth is 4. In fact, if Brandi's booth had a smaller number than 4, the problem would not work, as the music booth, stickers booth, and comics booth all have to have smaller numbers than the ice cream booth does. Thus, we can deduce that Brandi's ice cream booth is actually number 4.

This means that the music booth is number 3, and the sticker booth is number 2, and Kara's comics booth is number 1. Beyond this, there are no further conclusions that can be drawn or deductions that can be made. The following table/diagram reflects what is now known about the booths and their numbers:

Smallest Number

1.	Kara – Comics
2.	– Stickers
3.	– Music
4.	Brandi – Ice Cream
5.	Leno

Biggest Number

C is correct because the question asks which of the answer choices could be true. A cannot be true because the comics booth's number was 1. B cannot be true because the ice cream booth's number was 4. D cannot be true because Kara's booth's number was 1. E cannot be true because the music booth's number was 3.

24. **(F)** For "decoding sentence" question types, try to figure out what as many of the letters mean as possible.

Here, the third sentence contains the word "Katie," so it is necessary to focus on this sentence and find comparisons. Looking at the other sentences, it becomes apparent that the first sentence and the third share 4 words and 4 coded letters: "Mick," "sings," "a," and "song"; and X, L, O, and R. Given that there are only 5 words in a sentence, it should fairly quickly become obvious that the letter representing "Katie" is Y.

25. **(A)** To answer this question, it is important to decode as many of the words as we can. It was already established that "Katie" is Y. We can also deduce that "a" is represented by O, by looking at the fourth sentence. And by looking at the second sentence, we can ascertain that P represents "happy." (You may have arrived at the same conclusion earlier when you were comparing the first and third sentences.)

By comparing the second and fourth sentences, it is possible to figure out that K represents "tune," since it was already established that O represents "a."

To recap, the words and their corresponding letters are as follows:

1. Katie – Y
2. a – O
3. happy – P
4. tune – K

The remaining words are:

1. Mick
2. sings
3. song
4. Chu
5. hums
6. Han
7. whistles
8. jolly

This makes A the correct answer, as there are still 8 words that cannot be completely decoded. For instance, the words "Mick," "sings," and "song" could be any of X, R, and L, but it is impossible to determine which letter represents which word.

READING ▶

READING

(Earthquakes)

26. **(K)** The passage details two catastrophic earthquakes and explains why the Richter scale was invented and how the scale works. The best choice is therefore K.

   F is incorrect. While the Richter scale alone cannot determine how much damage an earthquake can cause, it is still a good indicator of how catastrophe an earthquake can cause. Moreover, even if it was not a good indicator, F would still be wrong because that's not the purpose of the passage. G is incorrect because, while the author may venerate Richter for his invention, the purpose of the passage is not to praise him. H is incorrect because it is too narrow in scope. The passage does more than compare two earthquakes and their impacts. J is incorrect. The passage doesn't compare earthquakes with other natural disasters.

27. **(D)** In lines 29-31, the passage indicates that each point up on the Richter scale is tantamount to an energy release of 31.6 times. From 5.0 to 9.0, that's a 4-point increase on the Richter scale, which means that the energy output of an earthquake that registers 9.0 would be $(31.6)^4$, or approximately 1,000,000, times that of a 5.0 earthquake. In other words,

Earthquake (EQ) Strength Comparison	
Richter Scale	Relative Strength (compared to a 5.0 EQ)
5.0	–
6.0	31.6
7.0	31.6×31.6
8.0	$31.6 \times 31.6 \times 31.6$
9.0	$31.6 \times 31.6 \times 31.6 \times 31.6$

Without having to do very advanced math, the best way to approach this problem is to round 31.6 to 31 or even 30. $(30)^4 = 810,000$, which is closest to 1,000,000, so D is correct.

28. **(J)** Lines 44-51 provide the context for the answer to this question. The contributing factors to the destructiveness of an earthquake are listed by the passage as: the earthquake's strength, population density, geographic features, and architectural landscape. Thus, choices F, G, H, and K can be eliminated. One might argue that hypocenter location is relevant to the destructiveness of an earthquake, but keep in mind that the question is asking for the factor that isn't listed in the passage, not just for which are valid contributing factors.

29. **(C)** The first paragraph of the passage discusses the impact and consequences of the Chilean earthquake. It states in line 3 that over 1,600 were killed in Chile itself. Then the tsunami generated by the earthquake killed another 200 combined in Hawaii, Japan, and the Philippines. Thus, the correct answer is C.

   A may be tempting, but it is incorrect because it doesn't account for the 200 killed by the tsunami, which was caused by the earthquake. B is incorrect because it is the number directly injured by the earthquake, not the number killed. D is incorrect because that is the total of the number killed and injured directly the earthquake. E is incorrect because that's the number left homeless by the earthquake, but it is not the number of deaths the earthquake caused.

30. **(G)** To answer this question, it is best to go through a process of elimination.

   F is incorrect. While the passage does mention that strength of the earthquake is not the only factor that contributes to an earthquake's devastating potential, it does not hint that every earthquake, even microquakes, can cause devastating damage. H is incorrect because it assumes too much information that is not supported by the passage. For instance, may appear to be common sense that more lives would have been lost if the Haiti earthquake had been a 9.5 on the Richter scale and not a 7.0, but we don't know if millions of lives would have been lost. From the passage alone, it is impossible to determine what Haiti's population was like. We only know that the 7.0 earthquake caused 616,000 deaths and casualties, but we don't know if that number would have eclipsed a million if a larger earthquake had hit. J is incorrect. Granted, it may seem likely that a 9.0 earthquake would cause tsunamis, when possible. But it may be possible that a 9.0 earthquake does not generate any tsunamis, such as if the earthquake happened in the middle of a large continent. K is incorrect because it assumes too much, as well. Lines 9-10 indicate that the tsunami alone caused over half a billion dollars' worth of damage. It may be reasonable to assume that the earthquake itself caused over half a billion dollars in damages. What is not indicated, however, is if the damage caused by the earthquake directly resulted in damage worth over $1.5 billion.

(Roald Amundsen)

31. **(E)** This passage discusses Roald Amundsen's adventures and accomplishments, particularly as a polar explorer. It focuses on how he was the first to achieve multiple feats. E is therefore the best answer choice.

A is incorrect. The passage does not compare Amundsen to major explorers and advocate for his increased recognition and fame. B is incorrect. Peary may have falsified his travel data, but that is not what the passage is about, as a whole. C is incorrect. While the statement may generally be agreeable, it is too general of a statement to be the main idea of this passage. D is incorrect for a couple of reasons. First, in the off chance that Peary didn't falsify his data, then Amundsen would not be the first to reach the North Pole. Second, even if Amundsen were the first to reach the North Pole, that's not the bulk of what the passage is about.

32. **(G)** The answer to this question lies in lines 10-13. They state that Amundsen knew from an early age that he would embark on polar

explorations. This knowledge prompted him to condition himself for arctic climates by sleeping with his window open at nights. F is incorrect because the passage does not state or infer that Amundsen trained for polar expeditions by accompanying his parents on overseas expeditions. H is incorrect for a similar reason. J is incorrect. While Amundsen did study other explorers' journeys (in lines 34-36, the passage states that Amundsen studied as much of Shackleton's South Pole attempt as possible), he did not do so at an early age to train for polar expeditions. K is incorrect because there is no mention in the passage of Amundsen gradually increasing the difficulty of his expeditions. Furthermore, there is no indication that the Northwest Passage was easier than Antarctica.

33. **(C)** The correct answer for this question can be found in lines 22-26. They state that scholars realized Peary's described route and timeframe for getting to the North Pole were nigh impossible. Thus, C is correct.

A is incorrect because it is too strong of a statement. Nigh impossible does not mean impossible. The phrase "even if he had flown there by airplane" should set off warning bells that this answer choice is incorrect because it is extraneous information. B is incorrect. The passage never states that Peary admitted to falsifying his records or that he admitted that Amundsen was the first to reach the North Pole. D is incorrect because the information stated within is not found in the passage. E is incorrect because there had to have been ships that could sail through polar waters, in order for explorers to go on polar expeditions. Even if that's not something we can assume, E would still be incorrect because it is not stated by the passage.

34. **(F)** F is correct because Roald Amundsen was not the first to reach Antarctica, so it is the least supported statement. Lines 31-34 indicate that at least one other expedition, Shackleton's, had reached Antarctica before Amundsen did, although Shackleton did not make it to the South Pole.

G is incorrect because it may have been possible that Amundsen would not have sailed to Antarctica if he had known Peary's records were falsified. He may have chosen to set sail for the North Pole, and if another party succeeded in reaching the South Pole first, he may never have set sail for Antarctica. H is incorrect; the passage states in lines 7-8 that Amundsen was born in 1862. Then, in lines 13-15, the passage states that Amundsen laid eyes on Antarctica's glacial walls for the first time in 1897. This would have made him either 34 or 35. J is incorrect; Shackleton's expedition probably encountered mishaps on its way to the South Pole. The passage states that the expedition was "*forced* to turn back just 97 miles short of the South Pole," in lines 32-33. K is incorrect; lines 39-44 state that Amundsen set out from the Bay of Whales on October 18. Almost two months later, on December 14, the team raised the Norwegian flag at the South Pole.

35. **(A)** A is the correct answer for a couple of reasons. Upon learning that Peary had reached the North Pole, which had been Amundsen's original goal, Amundsen abandoned that course of action, instead focusing his efforts on sailing to Antarctica (lines 18-27). Also, in lines 15-17, it states that Amundsen wanted to be the first to set foot on Antarctica. And then, in lines 45-47, the passage states that Amundsen became the first to fly over the North Pole in a dirigible. These facts, taken together, indicate that Amundsen wanted to be the first to accomplish some sort of exploration feat.

B is incorrect because it is unknown whether Amundsen would have become clinically depressed if was denied the chance at being first to the South Pole. C is incorrect because, strictly based on the passage alone, it cannot be determined if Amundsen had prepared for his trip to Antarctica for more than a year. All that is told is that he began making preparations for the North Pole in 1909 and that he set out for Antarctica in the June of 1910. It is not specified when in 1909 Amundsen began preparing for Antarctica.

D is incorrect; there is not enough information to support the conclusion or assumption that Amundsen was the one who gave the Bay of Whales its name. E is incorrect because there is not enough information. (And though the passage doesn't mention it, the airplane had been invented by the time Amundsen flew over the North Pole.)

(Right to Bear Arms)

36. **(J)** The purpose of this passage is not to urge any sort of action involving gun control or the repeal of the Second Amendment, which rules out F as an answer choice. Rather, the purpose of this passage is to provide a possible explanation as to why guns are so prevalent in American culture. The justification for J is found in lines 11-16 and 39-47.

Choice H may be tempting, but it is incorrect because the language is too strong. This passage isn't trying to prove anything. The purpose is to conjecture and theorize.

37. **(B)** The answer to this question is quite straightforward. Lines 26-29 indicate that Mary and William of Orange deposed of King James II in 1688, which makes B the correct answer.

38. **(H)** Here, H is the best answer because the passage states, in lines 32-35, that the English Bill of Rights was designed to correct the abuses of power by King James II and to better define and guarantee the rights of the English people. And since William and Mary were required to accept the Bill of Rights, this means that the English Bill of Rights was designed to prevent future abuses of power.

F is not supported by the passage. While it is certainly possible that the English Bill of Rights prevented the government to engage in taxation without representation, there is no mention of it in the passage. Therefore, G is incorrect. J is incorrect; it is not mentioned in the passage, either. K is incorrect because the English Bill of Rights was designed to better define and guarantee the rights of the English people, not partially guarantee and protect the Englishmen's rights.

39. **(C)** Lines 17-25 of the passage indicate that King James II was not an absolute monarch. He made moves to become one, which caused greater tension with Parliament. This indicates that James had to share power with Parliament.

A is incorrect. The passage does not support the conclusion that Parliament would have taken over the monarch's authority, in addition to the authority that it already had. As we see, Parliament looked for another monarch instead. B is incorrect; it assumes that American colonists were solely influenced by the English Bill of Rights in their determination of what rights should be guaranteed and protected, and such an assumption is not supported. D is incorrect. While it might have been possible that the United States would have been an extension of Britain, had it not been for King George's oppression of the colonists, the passage is not saying trying to suggest this. It is merely establishing that King George's oppression definitely propelled the American colonists to rebellion. E is incorrect; it cannot be ascertained what fraction of the English were Protestants.

40. **(K)** Lines 24-29 suggest that William and Mary were connected to Parliament. The sentence ending in line 26 states that King James II caused additional tension with Parliament. This tension culminated in King James's deposition. If William and Mary weren't connected to Parliament, it wouldn't make sense that the tension felt by Parliament resulted in the deposition of the king by William and Mary. Thus, K is correct.

F is not supported by the passage. The author would probably agree with the statement that mass killings would be reduced if guns were made unavailable to the public, but it is too strong of a statement to say that mass killings would forever cease if guns were made unavailable publicly, as other weapons could be

used. G is incorrect. The author may very well believe that guns, when used correctly, can aid in self-defense or the defense of others. Beware of strong language such as "forever," and "no." H is incorrect. In lines 6-8, the passage cites a survey that showed that the United States had an average of 90 guns per every 100 citizens. This does not mean 90% of citizens own guns. Some people may own more guns than others, thereby causing the average to go up. J is incorrect. James may not have been overthrown if he had not promoted Catholicism, but it is also possible that his other actions would have resulted in his overthrow; there isn't enough information to support one conclusion or the other.

(Stephen King)

41. **(B)** This passage is about Stephen King and provides a glimpse into how he is able to write so prolifically. It starts out with background information about King and wraps up with a discussion of how he is able to write so much. Thus, B is the correct answer. The other answer choices are too narrow in scope to be correct.

42. **(K)** The answer to this question lies in lines 35-38. Genre, writing style, personal circumstances, and philosophical approaches all contribute to how quickly an author is able to write and his or her commercial success. Thus, K is the correct answer because level of family support is not listed. Again, it is important to remember the passage is asking for what is stated and not what is reasonable.

43. **(A)** Lines 42-44 indicate that Stephen King is prolific because he commits to writing 1,500 words per day. Thus, A is correct.

B draws an improper conclusion. While he was an English major, it is not necessarily because he was an English major that he is a prolific writer. C is not stated or suggested by the passage. D is incorrect because only half of it is true. In line 42, Stephen King is quoted as saying that he is not a fast writer. E is incorrect because, even if true, his natural writing talent is not by itself the reason he can write prolifically.

44. **(G)** G is correct. Lines 24-30 state that Harper Lee's To Kill a Mockingbird won the Pulitzer Prize and became a staple in English curricula all around the country. That speaks to the novel's literary success. Commercially, the novel sold over 30 million copies.

F is incorrect. Harper Lee was not a more prolific writer, having published one book in her lifetime, whereas Stephen King has published over 60 (lines 2-3). H, J, and K are incorrect because they are unsupported by the passage. For instance, *To Kill a Mockingbird* is a commercial and literary success, but the passage does not draw any comparisons between Harper Lee's novel and any of Stephen King's. And it may be true that declaring an author to be successful is somewhat of a flawed process, but it is not mentioned in or implied by the passage.

45. **(D)** Lines 18-22 indicate that throughout college, Stephen King began writing and selling his short stories. The first short story he sold was "The Glass Door" in 1967. He sold it to the publication group *Startling Mystery Stories*. *Startling Mystery Stories* was not the title of his work, so D is correct.

(Investment)

46. **(F)** The purpose of this passage is to introduce various investment vehicles and discuss the risks involved with investing and how to minimize that risk. Thus, F is the correct answer. G is incorrect. While the passage distinguishes between the various types of securities, the passage also does more than just distinguish between the various types of securities. It also discusses and defines key investment terms; but again, this is not the main purpose of the passage. As a result, H is incorrect. J is incorrect; the passage does not advocate investment. It only attempts to provide more information about some aspects of investments. K is incorrect; the passage does not try to alert readers to possible incorrect information they may have.

47. **(E)** Lines 1-12 and 20-21 contain support for the answer to this question. The passage indicates that real estate acquisitions, savings accounts, certificates of deposit, business startup involvement, and securities are all investment vehicles. And stocks, bonds, and mutual funds are all types of securities. E is therefore right.

48. **(J)** Lines 13-17 indicate that there are several factors that determine risk, but it explicitly states that the biggest risk is the investor himself. J is therefore the correct answer. The factors stated in the other answer choices could be or are contributing to investment risk, but they are not expressly stated to be the greatest risk.

49. **(A)** According to the passage, in lines 21-27, bonds are equivalent to loans, so the investor has an expectation of being paid back what he invested, plus interest. They are, in other words, debt obligations; the company issuing the bonds is in debt to the investor. Stocks, the passage states, are ownership interests in the company. A is therefore correct.

50. **(H)** Diversification is defined in lines 33-37. It is the act of investing in various securities to minimize the risk of loss, in the event that the value of one or more investments drops.

F is incorrect because the passage does not state that diversification is a way for investors to not conduct careful research. Furthermore, lines 41-48 state that investors should carefully study and analyze stocks in order to reduce the risks of investing. Nor is diversification a guarantee against stock price volatility; it helps diffuse risk. Thus, G is incorrect. J and K are incorrect because there is no mention of investor greed and better opportunities for small companies.

MATH EXPLANATIONS ▶

Answer Explanations – Mathematics
Practice Test 3

51. **(E)** To solve this problem, use the process of elimination.

   A is incorrect because, if y is negative, then x would be positive.

   B is incorrect because, if y is positive, then x would be negative.

   C is incorrect. Rearranging the inequality, we get $2y \geq x^2 - x$ or $2y \geq y^6 + y^3$, after substituting $^-y^3$ in for x. After dividing each side by y, we get $2 \geq y^5 + y^2$. If y is a positive number, for instance, then the inequality does not work, so C cannot be the correct answer.

   D is incorrect because $x - y^3$ leads to $^-2y^3$, which means that the expression will be positive if y is negative and negative if y is positive.

   E is correct because the sum of a number and its additive inverse is always 0.

52. **(G)** The sum of the height of all 7 boys is:

   $7 \times 63 = 441$ inches

   Since Byron's height is 72 inches, the combined height of the other boys is $441 - 72 = 369$ inches.

53. **(A)** If Marcia is 11 now, 9 years ago, she was 2 years old. And if Winona was 3 times as old as Marcia was then, that means 9 years ago, Winona was 6 years old. This leads to the conclusion that Winona is 15 years old now.

54. **(K)** If Benny has 5 different pens, he can arrange them in 120 ways.

   There are 5 pens he can choose for the first pen. Thereafter, he can choose 4 pens, 3 pens, 2 pens, and then 1 pen. You multiply 5 by 4 by 3 by 2 by 1 to get the answer.

   Why do you multiply these numbers?

   If, for instance, you had 5 different pens, and you wanted to choose a pen, you would have 5 options for your first pen. Once you've selected a pen, you have 4 pens left to choose from. Since are 4 pens left to choose from after each of the 5 possible first pens you chose, there would be 20 different ways to pair 2 pens out of 5. Extend this logic to the next 3 pens, and you can see why you multiply 5, 4, 3, 2, and 1 for this problem.

55. **(C)** The factors of 66 are: 1, 2, 3, 6, 11, 22, 33, 66.

   The sum of these numbers are: 144, which is 12 squared.

56. **(J)** Distribute $4z$ across the terms in the parentheses to get $28zq - 24zw$.

57. **(A)** If a customer had $90,000.00 in her bank account, she would earn $2,700.00 in interest: $90,000 \times .03 = 2,700$.

   If the customer had 100,000.00 in her savings account, she would earn $2,500.00 in interest: $100,000 \times .025 = 2,500$.

   She would thus earn $200 more in interest by having $90,000 as opposed to $100,000.

58. **(J)** To start, realize that 2,310 can be broken down into 231×10.

The factors of 231 are: 1, 3, 7, 11, 21, 77, 231.

The factors of 10 are: 1, 2, 5, 10

We see that the greatest prime factor of 2,310 is 11, while the least prime factor is 2. The difference is therefore 9.

Interesting Fact: If the sum of the digits of a number is a multiple of 3, then the number is divisible by 3.

59. **(E)** There are several different approaches possible to solve this problem. Worked out below is just one way:

After multiplying 2 and ¼, you get ½, which is 0.5. Subtract your result from 3 to get 2.5. 2.5 divided by 0.5 gives you 5.

$$\frac{3 - 0.5}{0.5} = \frac{2.5}{0.5} = \frac{25}{5} = 5$$

60. **(G)** The logger can cut a log into 2 pieces in 4 minutes, meaning it takes him 4 minutes to make 1 cut.

In order for the logger to cut a log into 6 pieces, he needs to make 5 cuts. With each cut taking 4 minutes, he'll need 20 minutes to cut a log into 6 pieces.

61. **(B)** To convert seconds into hours, do the following:

$$225 \text{ sec} \times \frac{1 \text{ min}}{60 \text{ sec}} \times \frac{1 \text{ hr}}{60 \text{ min}}$$

$\frac{225}{3,600}$ or 0.0625 hours is correct.

62. **(G)** If there are 4 girls to 3 boys at a camp, that means the total number of campers was a multiple of 7. The ratio of girls to campers is therefore 4 to 7.

Expressed as a fraction, the ratio 4 to 7 is $\frac{4}{7}$, which is 0.5714 as a decimal or 57.14%.

63. **(A)** If Kirk and Sofia start at the same point on the track but run in opposite directions until they meet, by the time they meet, they will have covered the entirety of the track. In other words, the sum of the distances each runs will be 1,300 feet.

$D_T = D_K + D_S = 1,300$ feet, where D_T is the total distance run, D_K is the distance Kirk runs, and D_S is the distance Sofia runs.

Further break down the individual distances by using the distance formula of $d = r \times t$ (distance equals rate × time):

$$D_K = R_K \times T$$

$$D_S = R_S \times T$$

(Note: T is the same for Kirk and Sofia, since they ran for the same amount.)

Furthermore, $R_K = 1.5 \times R_S$. Since T is equivalent for Kirk and Sofia, $D_K = 1.5 \times D_S$, by substitution. This leads to:

$$(1.5 \times D_S) + D_S = 2.5 \times D_S = 1,300 \text{ feet}$$

$$D_S = 520 \text{ feet} \rightarrow D_K = 780 \text{ feet}$$

64. **(H)** If the smallest of 8 consecutive odd integers is k, the integers can be written as:

$k, k + 2, k + 4, k + 6, k + 8, k + 10, k + 12,$ and $k + 14$

In this case, the median is the average of $k + 6$ and $k + 8$, or $k + 7$.

65. **(E)** Rearrange the equation so that x is by itself on one side:

$3x = {}^-15y + 3$

Divide both sides by 3 to get x by itself:

$x = {}^-5y + 1$

Multiply both sides by 2:

$2x = {}^-10y + 2$

Add 1 to both sides:

$2x + 1 = {}^-10y + 3$

---

66. **(H)** To solve this problem, go through a process of elimination.

- $f(x) + g(x) = (4x - 1) + (5x + 2) = 9x + 1$

If x is even, then $9x + 1$ is odd, which makes F incorrect.

- $g(x) - f(x) = (5x + 2) - (4x - 1) = x + 3$

If x is odd, then $x + 3$ is even, so G is incorrect. J is indeed the correct answer. For any positive x, $x + 3$ will be positive.

- $f(x) - g(x) = (4x - 1) - (5x + 2) = {}^-x - 3$

Any positive value of x will produce a negative value for ${}^-x - 3$, so J is incorrect.

- $f(x) \times g(x) = (4x - 1) \times (5x + 2)$
  $= 20x^2 + 3x - 2$

The expression $20x^2 - 2$ will always be even, but if x is odd, then $3x$ will be odd. Thus, if x is odd, $f(x) \times g(x)$ is odd, and so K is wrong.

67. **(D)** First, find the values of the square roots:

$\sqrt{5^2} = 5$ and $\sqrt{6^2} = 6$, while $\sqrt{5^2 + 6^2} = \sqrt{61}$. $\sqrt{61}$ falls between 7 and 8, since $8^2 = 64$.

Thus, the sum of the square roots in the problem is between 18 and 19.

---

68. **(G)** This question is asking you to find the perimeter of the figure.

The perimeter of the two semicircles adds up to the circumference of one:

$C = 2\pi r$, which in our case is 6π cm.

We know that the sides of the square are 10 cm each. Ordinarily, the ant would have to walk 40 cm around the square, but 12 cm of the sides of the square are covered by the semicircles. The total distance along the square itself is thus $40 - 12 = 28$ cm.

Take the sum of the semicircles' perimeter and the perimeter of the portion of the square that's not covered by the semicircles to get:

$28 + 6\pi$ cm

---

69. **(D)** First, evaluate a and b individually.

$a = (16) \div (4) = 4$

$b = 7 + 1 - 5 = 3$

Then multiply a and b:

$a \times b = 4 \times 3 = 12$

70. (K) Figuring out the individual segments lengths will help solve this problem.

$RU = RS + SU = 12$ cm

$RS = SU \rightarrow RS = SU = 6$ cm

From this, we can find ST, TU, and UV. For ST and TU:

$SU = ST + TU = 6$ cm

Since $TU = 2(ST)$,

$TU = 4$ cm, and $ST = 2$ cm

For UV:

$SV = SU + UV$

$20 = 6 + UV \rightarrow UV = 14$ cm

Thus, $TU - ST + UV = 4 - 2 + 14 = 16$ cm.

---

71. (E) There is a 50% chance of Nate getting an even number every time he rolls. The easiest way to solve this problem is to figure out the probability of Nate not getting 2 evens and subtracting this probability from 1, where 1 represents 100%. (The probability of Nate getting at least 2 even rolls is equal to the sum of the probabilities of getting 2, 3, 4, and 5 even rolls.)

The probability that Nate doesn't get 2 evens can be broken down into the probability that Nate doesn't get any evens P(0E) and the probability that Nate gets 1 even P(1E).

$$P(0E) = P(6O) = \left(\frac{1}{2}\right)^5 = \frac{1}{32}$$

Finding the probability of Nate getting 1 even is a little trickier. There are essentially two ways of approaching this. The first, more advanced way is to say:

$$P(1E) = \binom{5}{1}\left(\frac{1}{2}\right)^5, \text{ where}$$

$$\binom{5}{1} = \frac{5!}{(1!)(4!)} = \frac{5 \times \cancel{4 \times 3 \times 2 \times 1}}{(1)(\cancel{4 \times 3 \times 2 \times 1})} = 5$$

This would mean that $P(1E) = \dfrac{5}{32}$.

Another way to find the probability of getting 1 even is to draw a chart. If he rolls the die 5 times, but only 1 roll can be even:

1	2	3	4	5
E	O	O	O	O
O	E	O	O	O
O	O	E	O	O
O	O	O	E	O
O	O	O	O	E

This shows that there are 5 different ways to get 1 even, if he rolls the die 5 times.

For each row, the probability of getting the exact sequence shown is 1/32—remember that the probability of getting an even is ½, but so is the probability of getting an odd on a roll. There are 5 possible rows that depict where an even roll could pop up, so we say:

$$5 \times \frac{1}{32} = \frac{5}{32}$$

The probability of getting at least 2 evens:

First, the sum of P(0E) and P(1E) is

$$\frac{6}{32} = \frac{3}{16}.$$

The probability of getting at least 2 even rolls is then:

$$1 - \frac{3}{16} = \frac{13}{16}$$

72. **(H)** It is tempting to say that the average speed is 55 miles per hour, since that's the average of 50 and 60. This is, however, erroneous.

Apply the *distance = rate × time* formula to her total trip. But, first, we must find how long it took Margot to drive to the resort and how long it took her to drive back.

Driving to the resort:

$d = rt$ → $450 = 50t$ → $t = 9$ hours

Driving back:

$450 = 60t$ → $t = 7.5$ hours

Thus, Margot's total driving time is 16.5 hours. She drove a total of 900 miles, going both ways, so:

$900 = 16.5r$ → $r = 54.54$ miles per hour

---

73. **(A)** $X + Y = 180$, and $X + Z = 90$. All that can be established by these facts is that X is less than 90, which means Y has to be greater than 90. Thus, angle Y is obtuse.

---

74. **(F)** To solve this problem, simply perform the operations required:

25% of 16 = $0.25 × 16 = 4$

16% of 25 = $0.16 × 25 = 4$

The sum is 8, which is 50% of 16.

---

75. **(C)** If Lenny has 2 dimes, Ted has 8 dimes, which totals $1.00. There is then $6.75 in quarters between Lenny and Ted, so set up a system of equations to find the quarters:

$6.75 = 0.25L + 0.25T$

$L = 2T$ → $6.75 = 0.75T$ → $T = 9$, $L = 18$

76. **(F)** If the area of circle O is 16π, the radius of circle O is 4, which in turns means that the side length of square in which it is inscribed is 8. The area of the square is 64.

The shaded area of the region outside of circle O, but still in the bigger square can be found by:

Area of square – Area of circle:

$64 - 16\pi$ in^2

To find the area of the shaded region inside the circle, first find the area of one of the shaded triangles, whose sides are radii of the circle:

Area of triangle = $\frac{1}{2}bh = \frac{1}{2} × 4 × 4 = 8$ in^2

Since there are 2 such triangles, the total shaded region inside circle O is 16 in^2.

Thus the total shaded region has an area of: $64 - 16\pi + 16 = 80 - 16\pi$ in^2

---

77. **(D)** First, simplify the equation by multiplying each side of the equation by 5. This leaves us with:

$7r - 2p = 40p$ → $7r = 42p$ → $r = 6p$

This means that $r^2 = 36p^2$

$3r^2 = 108p^2$

---

78. **(J)** If Wilfred placed a sticky note on every third page of his notebook, starting with page 1, then he placed sticky notes on pages according to the following formula: $3n - 2$, with n representing the nth sticky note Wilfred places.

The last sticky note Wilfred can place is on page 298. This would mean that Wilfred can place 100 sticky notes. $3(100) - 2 = 298$.

79. (B) The easiest way to solve this problem is to construct a rectangle around the triangle with coordinates of:

(-5, -4), (-5, 4), (7, 4), and (7, -4)

Notice that by drawing this rectangle, three other rectangles appear. Finding the areas of those rectangles and subtracting their sum from the area of the rectangle is simpler than directly trying to find the area of the triangle given by the problem.

In other words: Area of rectangle – Sum of the areas of the three triangles = Area of triangle given by the problem.

The area of the rectangle:

Area of rectangle = 12 × 8 = 96

Let there be triangles I, II, and III. Let triangle I's coordinates be (-5, 4), (-5, -4), and (3, 4); triangle II's coordinates be (3, 4), (7, 4), and (7, -1); and triangle III's coordinates be (-5, -4), (7, -1), and (7, -4).

Triangle I: height = 8, base = 8; Area = 32
Triangle II: height = 5, base = 4; Area = 10
Triangle III: height = 3, base = 12; Area = 18

Sum of areas of triangles I, II, and III: 60

Then to find the area of the triangle given by the problem: 96 – 60 = 36.

80. (G) Convert the numbers from scientific notation to ordinary decimal numbers:

$1.56 \times 10^7 = 15,600,000$

$1.95 \times 10^6 = 1,950,000$

Then divide:

$$\frac{15,600,000}{1,950,000} = \frac{1,560}{195} = 8$$

81. (D) If 2 boats weighs the same as 3 cars, then 1 boat weighs the same as 1.5 cars. If the cargo jet can hold 79 boats, then it should be able to hold 79 × 1.5 cars = 118.5 cars. Thus, the cargo jet will be able to hold 118 whole cars.

82. (K) The surface area of a box is given by the formula:

$$S.A. = 2(l \times w) + 2(l \times h) + 2(h \times w)$$

Thus, applying the formula to our problem:

$$S.A. = 2(6 \times 13) + 2(6 \times 5) + 2(13 \times 5)$$

$$S.A. = 156 + 60 + 130 = 346 \text{ in}^2$$

83. (E) 9 years ago, Emil was 34 years old, which means Roderick was 17 years old then. Roderick is therefore 26 years old now. In 15 years, he will be 41 years old.

84. (J) If the ratio of the amount of homework Martin has left to do to the amount he has completed is 2 to 7, then the ratio of the amount of homework he completed to the amount of homework he received in the first place is 7 to 9. Expressing this ratio as a fraction, we get:

$\frac{7}{9}$, which is 77.778%, or 78% (rounded up).

85. (C) Draw a diagram and you should see that the total area the bobcat has access to is equal to one-third of a circle with a radius of 24 feet, which is:

$$\text{Area} = \frac{1}{3} \times \pi (24)^2 = \frac{\overset{8}{24} \times 24 \times \pi}{\cancel{3}_1} = 192\pi$$

86. (K) To solve this problem, the first step is to find the number of supporters of Plan A and Plan B:

Plan A: $0.63 \times 12,000 = 7,560$

Plan B: $0.74 \times 12,000 = 8,880$

$7,560 + 8,880 = 16,440$, which is more than the town's population. To find how many support both, use the following formula to find the intersection of people that support:

$A + B - AB$ = Population, where AB represent the people who support both.

$7,560 + 8,880 - AB = 12,000$

$AB = 16,440 - 12,000 = 4,440$

87. (B) The average age of the student's in Ms. Kim's class is:

$$\frac{13 + 11 + 10 + 12 + 12 + 11 + 10}{7} = 11.3$$

The average height in her class is:

$$\frac{60 + 53 + 54 + 63 + 58 + 57 + 53}{7} = 56.9$$

Thus, Wallace is the best choice.

88. (G) To solve this problem, all we have to do is set the expression equal to 5, as such:

$$\frac{1}{x} \times \frac{x+3}{2} = 5$$

After simplifying the left side of the equation to get $2x$ as the denominator, multiply both sides of the equation by $2x$:

$$x + 3 = 10x \rightarrow 9x = 3 \rightarrow x = \frac{1}{3}$$

89. (B) To solve this problem, first divide 2,500 by 6 to get 416 R4. This means that there were 416 groups of 6 people each, for a total of 2,496 people who were placed into groups. Since 3 people were left over without a group, the total attendance in the audience was 2,499.

90. (H) The length of the side of the square can be found by using the distance formula:

$$\text{Distance} = \sqrt{(x_2 - x_1)^2 + (y_2 - y_1)^2}$$

$$= \sqrt{(6-3)^2 + (4-0)^2}$$

$$= \sqrt{9+16} = 5$$

Thus, the area of the square is 5^2, or 25.

91. (B) There are 8 segments in the figure shown in the problem. That means it takes Al 3 minutes to run each segment.

To get to B for the 10th time, Al would have had to fully run the course 9 times first, which would amount to $24 \times 9 = 216$ minutes. Then, adding 3 segments, or 9 minutes, we get 225 minutes.

225 minutes is equal to $225 \times 60 = 13,500$ seconds.

92. (F) First set up the ratio of 4,000 : 32,000, since the problem is asking for the best estimate of the ratio, and not the exact ratio. Then divide each side by 4,000 to get the ratio of 1 : 8.

K seems like a good choice, but if you divide 31 by 4, you get a ratio of 1 : 7.75, whereas the ratio of the cars to the city's population is 1 : 7.99, rounding to the nearest hundredth.

93. (A) Otis walked a total of $5 + 3 + 7 + 7 = 22$ blocks to get to the arcade. Because

Otis walked 7 blocks south and 7 west from his friend's house, he is actually 2 blocks south and 4 blocks west of his house. Thus, he walks 6 blocks home. In total, Otis will walk 22 + 6 = 28 blocks.

---

94. **(G)** First, convert the yards to inches. 35 yd × 36 in/yd = 1,260 in. 40 yd × 36 in/yd = 1,440 in. Note that the ratio of 35 to 40 is 7 to 8 and that the ratio of 14 to 16 is also 7 to 8, which means this problem will work.

The ratio of 14 to 1,260 is 1 to 90. (The ratio of 16 to 1,440 is also 1 to 90.)

---

95. **(D)** The side length of square ABCD is 15 cm (the square root of 225 cm²). If the ratio of AE to ED is 2 to 1, AE is two-thirds of AD, which we know is 15 cm. This means AE is 10 cm, and ED is 5 cm.

Next, knowing that AB is 15 cm and AE is 5 cm, we can find BE by using the Pythagorean Theorem:

$(BE)^2 = 225 + 100 = 325$

$BE = \sqrt{325} = \sqrt{25 \times 13} = 5\sqrt{13}$

The perimeter of trapezoid BEDC is:

$15 + 15 + 5 + 5\sqrt{13}$ or

$35 + 5\sqrt{13} = 5(7 + \sqrt{13})$

---

96. **(K)** If the dimensions are increased by 400%, the new dimensions are 500% that of the original's. Thus, if the length and width of the original photograph are l and w, respectively, the new dimensions are $5l$ and $5w$. The area of the enlarged photograph is $25lw$, or 2,500% × lw.

---

97. **(E)** If 3 out of 8 shoppers are male, then 5 out of 8 are female. To find the total number of male and female shoppers:

$\dfrac{3}{8} \times 608 = 228$ male shoppers

$\dfrac{5}{8} \times 608 = 380$ female shoppers

$380 - 228 = 152$

---

98. **(F)** Substituting 11 in for x and 10 in for y, we get:

$(22 - 30)(30 + 22) = (^-8)(52) = {}^-416$

---

99. **(C)** PS = 14 − 8 = 6; WP = 8 − ⁻2 = 10

PS ÷ WP = 6 ÷ 10 = 0.6

---

100. **(J)** The probability of hitting the shaded region is:

$$P(S) = \frac{\text{Area of Shaded Region}}{\text{Total Area}}$$

There are two distinct shaded bands, the smaller band and the larger band.

Area of the smaller band = Area of the second circle − Area of the first circle: $9\pi - \pi = 8\pi$ in².

Area of the larger band = Area of the fourth circle − Area of the third circle: $49\pi - 25\pi = 24\pi$ in².

Thus, the total shaded area is $(8 + 24)\pi = 32\pi$ in².

The probability is thus: $\dfrac{32\pi}{49\pi} = \dfrac{32}{49}$

RESOURCES

WEBSITES

TJHSST Information[*]

School Homepage: www.tjhsst.edu

Admissions Page: www.fcps.edu/pla/TJHSST_Admissions/index.html

Application Information: www.fcps.edu/pla/TJHSST_Admissions/apply_freshman_winter.html

Testing Information: www.fcps.edu/pla/TJHSST_Admissions/apply_freshman_winter_testing.html

Selection Process: www.fcps.edu/pla/TJHSST_Admissions/dec_freshman_winter.html

Getting Ready Guide & Student Handbook: These can be found by going to the address below: http://www.fcps.edu/pla/TJHSST_Admissions/apply_freshman_winter_testing_getting%20ready.html

Note: You **must** type in all of the addresses **exactly** as shown, including the upper case letters. The Fairfax County Student Handbook contains 1 full-length practice test and explanations.

SHSAT Information[*]

SHSAT Information Page: schools.nyc.gov/Accountability/resources/testing/SHSAT.htm

Note: The SHSAT handbook contains 2 full-length practice tests and answer explanations.

Test Preparation Aides

Free Multiple Choice Answer Sheet: www.betterwritingcenter.com/publications.html

Free TJHSST Essay Practice Sheet: www.betterwritingcenter.com/publications.html

Originally, I considered including the multiple choice answer sheet and the essay practice sheet with this book, but I decided against that and instead made them downloadable. That way, you can download and print as many copies as you want.

---

[*] TJHSST and SHSAT information can easily be found by searching "tjhsst admissions" or "shsat" on the Bing or Google search engines.

BOOKS

SHSAT PREPARATION

Below are the books I frequently use to prepare my students for the TJAT. I have ranked them by my personal order of preference, according to a combination of various factors, such as the quality of the questions and problems presented within the books, the quantity of said questions and problems, and the prices of the books.

1. Won Suh's *SHSAT Practice Tests: NYC Edition* (available very soon after the time of this printing, if not concurrently with it)

2. Barron's *New York City SHSAT: Specialized High School Admissions Test*

3. McGraw-Hill's *New York City SHSAT*

4. Kaplan's *New York City Specialized High Schools Admissions Test*

5. Violet Dubinina's *Practice Math Tests for New York City SHSAT Specialized High School Admissions Test*, Volumes 1 and 2 (Note, these do not contain any verbal questions)

Practice Essay Prompts

Below is the list of prompts I have written and compiled to guide my TJAT prep students. The prompts are not ranked in any sort of order. I jot the prompts down whenever one comes to mind.

Directions: Read the following prompts carefully and prepare an appropriate response. Write with logical organization, clarity, and substance.

SIS PROMPTS

"Prompt" #0 – To be done prior to writing the SIS prompts

Assignment: List the activities, interests, and hobbies that you believe expounding on will help you get admitted to TJHSST. Write 4-6 sentences for each item you list, keeping in mind how it will help your chances of getting into TJ.

---

1. Describe an event or incident in your life that has given you great motivation or that has shaped your character in some profound way.

2. What can you contribute to the community of learners at TJHSST? In other words, how can you be an asset to TJHSST?

3. What do you see yourself doing in the future, and when and how did you decide on this potential career path?

4. Which role in a technology or applied math and sciences company--chief executive officer, chief operating officer, chief financial officer, researcher/engineer, project manager, or any other role that comes to mind--do you think best suits your personality and interests?

5. What does TJHSST uniquely offer that you are seeking and cannot easily obtain elsewhere? In other words, why are you applying to TJHSST?

6. TJHSST provides a challenging learning environment. What challenges or obstacles have you overcome that you believe will prepare you to face the obstacles presented by the rigor of TJHSST's curriculum?

7. It is expected that many students applying to TJHSST are at least somewhat passionate about a field or fields of STEM, but many students are also hardly so one-dimensional. What other fields of study or activities are you interested or participate in?

8. If you had to pick one word to describe you, what would it be and why?

ESSAY PROMPTS

1. *2016 UPDATE* You are the pilot of a medical evacuation helicopter. At 5:30 am, you receive word that a passenger on a cruise ship fell seriously ill and needs to be airlifted as quickly as possible to the nearest hospital. The cruise ship was 400 miles away from the nearest port, where your hospital is located, when the distress signal was sent, but it is making its way back to port at its maximum speed of 10 miles per hour.

   Your helicopter's fuel capacity is 6,600 pounds of fuel, and it burns 1,200 pounds of fuel per hour when it is airborne. The process of airlifting a passenger takes 30 minutes. Federal regulations stipulate that all medical evacuation helicopter pilots need to plan to retain at least an hour's worth of fuel at all times. If your helicopter flies at 150 miles per hour, at what time must you leave the hospital to get to the cruise ship passenger as quickly as possible?

2. *2015 UPDATE* What can schools do to make STEM more interesting to students? Prescribe a course or courses of action that can be implemented to increase the appeal of STEM to students.

3. *2014 UPDATE* A previously rare disease is now spreading through the United States. There is a vaccine for the disease, but there are limited supplies to treat the public since it was so previously rare.

   Who should decide who gets the vaccine first? If you were given the authority to make that decision, whom would you give the vaccine to first? Explain your answers.

4. Is honesty always the best policy?

5. What role do ethics play in the workplace?

6. Do humans have a duty to be considerate of others? Explain.

7. What is the most important trait for a leader to have?

8. Is it sometimes better to be selfish, or should we always be as selfless as possible?

9. Do ends always justify the means?

10. Describe a time or incident when you persevered to overcome a significant hurdle or challenge.

11. Describe a time or incident when you used creativity to overcome a significant hurdle or challenge.

12. Define teamwork and explain its importance.

13. Is it possible for humanity to become too dependent on technology?

14. You saw someone in a predicament crying out for help. When you were in a similar predicament in the past, however, the same person deliberately ignored your pleas for help. How do you respond to this person's present pleas?

15. Ultimately, is passion or discipline more valuable?

16. If you could go back in time and eliminate an invention or technology, what would it be?

17. What does success mean to you?

18. There is an adage which says, "Every cloud has a silver lining." Do you agree or disagree with it?

19. Should we ordinary citizens be allowed to take the law into our own hands, if the criminal justice system is not doing an adequate job?

20. If you could choose to eliminate poverty or illiteracy, which would you choose and why?

21. We are all familiar with the maxim, "The pen is mightier than the sword." In a tightly integrated essay, briefly explain this maxim and then explain if you agree or disagree with it.

22. We are all familiar with the saying, "Sticks and stones may break my bones, but words will never hurt me." Briefly explain this saying and then explain if you agree or disagree with it.

23. You are on a soccer team that has just secured its spot in the league championship game. However, the night before the championship game, you found out a player on your team got on to the team by cheating the league's rules and regulations. This player, however, is your team's most valuable player and your chances of winning the championship game are diminishingly slim without him. Needless to say, if you report him, he will be eliminated from the game. Do you report the MVP or not?

    a. Suppose, however, that if you report him, your team will be eliminated from the championship game without being given a chance of contending, even without the MVP. Further suppose that many of your teammates are enthralled just to be playing in the championship game, since it's a great opportunity and learning experience; they are not concerned with winning and just want to be able to play in the championship game. Do you report the MVP or not?

24. In order to protect its citizens against the outbreaks of deadly viruses, the government has commissioned a scientist to develop a super vaccine to counteract all viruses. The scientist discovered during the testing phase that the vaccine would immunize 99.99% of society. Unfortunately, however, he found that people with a certain genetic trait (those comprising the remainder 0.01%), and just that genetic trait, would die. Should the government, assuming it knows about the scientist's findings, allow the vaccine to be distributed to the public?

    How does your analysis change, if at all, if:

    a. the vaccine killed off 0.01% of the population, but without discrimination (meaning it kills people off but without any particular pattern or order)?

b. the vaccine has been determined to be the most theoretically perfect vaccine creatable (but it still kills off the 0.01% of the population with the certain genetic trait), and as such it is impossible to create a better vaccine?

25. A television show is rated TV-14, which means that the contents of the program are intended for viewers aged 14 years or older. The creators and writers of the show realize that younger audiences make up a significant portion of the show's viewers. Select one of the following choices and present your argument accordingly:

26. If you could talk to anyone, even historical figures, about anything, whom would you talk to and what would you talk about and why?

27. Do you agree or disagree with the saying "You can't teach an old dog new tricks"?

28. When we are faced with an impossible challenge, hurdle, or obstacle, is it better to struggle to the bitter end in the hopes we will prevail or to cut our losses at some point and move on?

29. If you could do one thing in your life again differently, what would it be and why and how would you do it differently?

30. If you could impart one message or life lesson, what would it be and why?

31. Whom do you consider a role model or hero? Explain.

32. Pick an invention and discuss its societal impact and significance. Some suggestions are: the light bulb, internet, telephone, computer, automobiles, airplane, refrigeration, nuclear power, and sewer/sewage system

33. You and a friend are applying for positions at a prestigious summer internship. This requires all applicants not only to submit a resume but also to take an aptitude test. You notice that your friend's resume is stronger than the majority of the other candidates'. You know that your friend would do as well as, if not better than, most of the other interns who would be selected. However, you know that your friend is a terrible test taker. Your friend has asked you to let her cheat off of you on the test just this once so you guys can have the internship together; without your friend, you wouldn't know anyone else at the internship. The only penalty for getting caught is not being selected for the internship, and there is almost zero chance of getting caught, because of the way the test is proctored. What do you do, and why?

34. Is defeat a better teacher than victory?

35. A fire is currently devastating the forests of a national park. Thousands of acres of trees have been severely scorched. Firefighters are debating the use of a newly proposed fire retardant to quell the fire. The retardant will put the fire out more quickly, but it has not been tested enough for scientists to figure out the possible environmental consequences of its use, whereas the retardant currently being used has been deemed moderately safe for the environment. Should the firefighters use the newly proposed retardant?

SAMPLE ESSAY RESPONSES

Below are two essays I wrote to answer two of the prompts. They are not intended to be masterpieces by any means; I wrote them solely to better help students understand about organization, flow, and style.

Prompt #30 Response

If a friend asked me to let him cheat off of me on the aptitude test for a summer internship, I would say no. It wouldn't be an easy choice to make, to be sure, but it would be the necessary one. There's a lot at stake, and I could very well jeopardize my friendship by refusing to let him cheat off me. He would definitely get upset and maybe refuse to talk to me ever again. It could mean the end of the friendship. The question to ask is, "Is standing up for your integrity worth the risk of your best friendship?" The answer to that question is a difficult yes.

On the one hand, my friend is highly qualified for the internship position, so helping him wouldn't even be cheating in the sense that it would be helping him get something he didn't deserve or something he'd be bad at. If anything, he would deserve it more than a lot of the other applicants. It's not his fault that he's a bad test taker, and for that reason I'd want to help him out. Not to mention, I'd have a better time with him there than if he wasn't.

But on the other hand, how would I feel about myself at the end of the day? More than my fear of getting caught is how guilty I'd feel. Even though my friend is just as qualified for the position, he'd still have gotten it unfairly. Part of getting the internship is how well you take the test, not just how smart you are and how well you would do at the internship. I'd feel guilty because I'd know that there are many other candidates who tried their best in an honest and fair way, but they wouldn't get the position because of me. Furthermore, if my friend can't overcome his bad test taking skills, he'll have much bigger problems later on than just an internship. He'll have problems with colleges and jobs. Is it my job to help him cheat all of those times too?

It'd be a tough choice, deciding whether to let my friend cheat off me or not. But even if it means he'd feel betrayed, I wouldn't be able to let him, or else I'd feel like I could compromise my morals more easily later on and turn into a kind of person I don't want to be. Besides, if he really was best friend material, he'd understand.

Comments

This essay did not have the traditional 5-paragraph essay feel to it. In fact, there was no roadmap, and the hook is merged into the thesis. This essay still works because there is a good flow to it, and each body paragraph has a point that it makes, so the essay is still logically organized. This goes back to what I said before roadmaps not being imperative, especially when you're faced with a time crunch.

Prompt #29a Response

The advent of the internet was a revolution whose coup d'état was unlike any other which the world has seen before. No blood was shed, no lives lost, but the internet revolution was a movement arguably more powerful than any other before it. It crept up on us as a Trojan horse of sorts, coming into our lives apparently peaceably, but only to overthrow everything we knew about communication, productivity, and entertainment, with its greatly expedited information delivery system.

When the internet first started taking root in our daily lives, it did so with what we would now consider painfully slow internet connections. Slow as it was, it still allowed us to send messages and electronic versions of documents much more expeditiously than anything traditional postal mail could afford—the telephone was great for hearing people's voices immediately, but it was not possible to send documents over the telephone, so it had its limitations. Of course, there is still the need for traditional mail today. How else are we going to receive any physical item that we ordered online? It is undeniable, though, that the internet has completely altered the way we communicate, whether it's person to person or company to person. And now that we have moved past downloads speeds of 5 kilobytes per second to high-speed internet, such as cable and fiber optical internet, we can communicate in even more diverse ways.

The ability to receive and send information from a computer console further permitted a vast improvement in productivity technologies, allowing for far greater efficiency in our daily lives. Commerce, banking, investment, and education are among the areas of our lives that have been reshaped by the internet. Instead of having to leave our homes to purchase goods, we now have the option of having them delivered to our homes or workplaces. Instead of having to physically commute to a bank or other brick and mortar location—or having to wait days for a check to be delivered to its destination—to receive or transfer funds, we can do that online, using either our banks or sites such as PayPal. And instead of having to take exams on paper, many exams are becoming, or have already become, computerized. It is possible for students to submit homework assignments online (and to even do homework on an internet page) and to do research with greater expediency and facility, using the innumerable sources of information that have sprung up on the internet and continue to spring up at an astronomical rate.

On the flip side of productivity is entertainment. The internet has revolutionized the way we perceive entertainment. Everything from games, videos, and even music has been changed by the development and advancement of the internet. Before online gaming came into existence, people could either play games by themselves or with others, in person. With the rise of the internet, however, games have taken on a distinct social aspect: most games are now multiplayer with the ability to type or voice chat with fellow players. And, while videos were previously limited to movies, homemade videos, and music videos aired on television networks or watchable only on our televisions, the internet has brought with it creative new ways for us to watch all sorts of videos online, through online sites such as Netflix, Hulu, and YouTube. Similarly, the music industry has been radically altered because of the internet. Where, once, music could be bought only on physical media, music is now more widely distributed digitally over the internet, through peer-to-peer file sharing networks or internet retail sites.

The internet has brought with it both good and evil. Because it has allowed for far greater efficiency, it has served to amplify every aspect of our lives and of society. More good can be done with the internet, but so can more bad. Charity can be performed much more efficaciously, but so can criminal acts. The internet has irreversibly changed the world and will continue to change the world even more. We have already seen much change in the way we communicate, the way we conduct our day-to-day affairs, and the way we experience entertainment. As internet technology advances even more, we will watch our lives get shaped even more by the internet.

Comments

The response for prompt #29a was admittedly long. Even if you could write that much by hand in 30 minutes on the essay portion of the TJAT, the amount of space they give you to write would not permit such length. Your essay will be considerably shorter, so don't mind the length and word count. Rather, the point of this essay was to show you how to organize your essay.

The introduction had a hook; it discussed the impact of the invention of the internet. There was a thesis, which was, in a nutshell, that the advent of the internet was a revolution unlike anything the world had seen before because—and here comes the roadmap—it impacted the way we communicate, conduct our work, and entertain ourselves.

Following the introduction, the body paragraphs each focus on one of the supports mentioned by the introduction's roadmap. The first body paragraph was about communication, the second about productivity, and the third about entertainment. Did you also happen to catch the organization within the second and third body paragraphs, as well? Read the essay again carefully if you didn't.

The conclusion wraps up the essay and reiterates the key points made throughout the essay.

Note: There is some digression here, especially in the first body paragraph, which is normal for a first draft, but notice that I was able to bring the discussion back on track. If you happen to digress, make sure to either eliminate the digression or to at least bring your discussion back on track as quickly and fluidly as possible.

Made in the USA
Middletown, DE
13 August 2019